i

c

o

p

e

Praise for Jamie Iredell

"Iredell finds a way to blend the personal and the cultural in ways that are relevant, in ways that demand to be heard and remembered."
—**Roxane Gay, author of** *Bad Feminist*

"Jamie Iredell is one of the two or three best writers I know in this world. If you read him—you'll say the same thing. If you don't, that's fine. Your grandchildren will say it one day."
—**Scott McClanahan, author of** *Crapalachia*

"Iredell's unflinching candor cuts a bantering, conversational style . . . often interested in the messy and difficult aspects of life."
—**Publishers Weekly**

"His warts-and-all attitude to these whiskey-soaked disclosures may bring to mind Jack Kerouac or Charles Bukowski, though Iredell's confessional essays typically aim for more introspection and intellectual heft."
—**The Atlanta Journal-Constitution**

LAST MASS

—— JAMIE IREDELL

Also by Jamie Iredell

Prose. Poems. a Novel.
The Book of Freaks
I Was a Fat Drunk Catholic School Insomniac

Thanks to the editors of the following magazines, where parts of this book were first published or reprinted, sometimes in an altered form:

Anomalous Press, Berfrois, The Collagist, Continent, Everyday Genius, Freerange Nonfiction, Hobble Creek Review, The Literary Review, The Nervous Breakdown, Pear Noir!, Sleepingfish, Used Furniture Review.

Special thanks to the Hambidge Center Creative Residency Program.

And thanks to great help from great readers/writers: Christopher Bundy, Blake Butler, and Man Martin.

Special thanks to Michael J. Seidlinger, who took the risk.

This book would not be possible without my mother and father, without my brother and sister. And of course, nothing is possible without my girls: Sarah, Kinsey, and Bailey.

"*Su isla era la más fuerte de todo el mundo . . .*"
—a description of California, in *Las Sergas de Esplandian* (1510), the first known text to mention the name of my home state.

I am a Catholic. I was baptized Catholic as a baby, and Mom raised me as such. Dad converted, and became Catholic. My brother and sister are Catholics. Grandma and Grandpa were Catholics. My uncles are Catholic. My uncles' wives are Catholic. My cousins are Catholics. My aunt's husband's family is Catholic. His sisters' names are Faith, Hope, and Charity. I used to feel guilty after I masturbated. I am Catholic.

In the first Station of the Cross, Jesus—expressionless, haloed, his shoulders and wrists rope-bound—stands beside a scroll-wielding Pilot. No filth dirties the building. No age smudges the architecture. No raw sewage strews a gutter. Everything then was new, a world so new even the distant mountains sit wrinkleless. Roman soldiers jeer in the background. Said background is lavish: columns, drapes, blue sky, solitary cloud.

The highway's shoulders splashed green with Indian grass butting up against the asphalt and backed by white pines, red oaks, sycamores, maples, all rolling into the hills that gradually ascended into Georgia's Appalachian foothills and into the Appalachians themselves. The merest hint of autumn—splashes of yellow islands—hung out there in glimpses that my speed and gaps in the tree line along the highway afforded me of the forested countryside.

The priests baptized Miquel Josep Serra a Catholic, born 1713 in Petra, Mallorca. Twenty years before this birth, the Spanish Inquisition held *autos de fé* in Palma, Mallorca's capital, and Jews were burned at the stake. Four more *conversos* were burned in 1720, when Miquel was seven. For his Holy Orders, Miquel Josep adopted the name of one among Saint Francis's favorites, and he became Father Fray Junípero Serra, of the Order of Friars Minor. Later he became a *comisario* of the Holy Office of the Inquisition.

I went to the mountains of north Georgia, to a tiny cabin, so that I might write about how I am from California, and that Blessed Father Fray Junípero Serra was among the first people of European descent to set permanent feet in California. Like it was for the venerable Father's Native converts years ago, for me the Catholic Church, and my California past, and the me who I was when I went into these mountains—all of it—seemed an insurmountable bear.

Grizzly Man, Timothy Treadwell, got ate up by the bears he loved, his abdomen ripped open, the surrounding skin paled, his staring eyes vacant as the scream still etched across his face. Bowels and ribcage.

In photos I do tummy time on imitation sheepskin rugs, red-capped, two-toothed smile. I ramble my parents' backyard lawns, watering (or attempting to) the *Agapanthus*, poured into a denim short panted jumper, my hair brown and naturally blond highlighted, straight as a mop atop my head. Now the hair's curly and brown. I look very happy, happy little Catholic boy spilling his ice cream down a tiny dress shirt. Now I am dirty.

History knows little about Blessed Father Fray Junípero Serra's early years. His parents were farmers who kept up a hovel in Petra. The ground floor contained the future Apostle of California's bedroom and the animals' stable. Miquel Josep was sickly and small, growing to a mere five feet, two inches in adulthood—shorter than my wife. As eighteenth century things went, expectedly, Miquel Josep's siblings all died. The strongest presence in Mallorca was the Church. Franciscans founded the Lullian University in Palma, to which Miquel Josep applied. For having lived in Enlightenment Europe, Blessed Father Fray Junípero Serra's life and worldview was definitively medieval.

Blessed Father Fray Junípero Serra took his Doctor of Philosophy at the Lullian University, and there met two lifelong friends: Fathers Fray Francisco Palou and Juan Crespí, students. Together the three missioned to Nueva España then to Baja California, and finally to Alta California. They would found nine missions in what is today the American State of California. At Blessed Father Fray Junípero Serra's deathbed Father Fray Francisco Palou administered extreme unction and last rites. Father Fray Junípero Serra would be buried beside the already-deceased Father Fray Juan Crespí, where together they still lie, beneath the bronze sarcophagus and the stone floor of La Basílica de San Carlos de Borromeo, in Carmel, California, the city in which I was born.

In high school I took girls to Mission San Carlos. The courtyard draped with bougainvillea and African daisies, the fountains gurgling in tune with the swallows' songs. I knew a stone bench recessed in a bower of roses. There's nothing like Catholicism for drawing out teenagers' urges.

Father Fray Junípero Serra founded La Misión de San Diego de Alcalá, around which grew the City of San Diego; and La Misión de San Carlos de Borromeo—Monterey; and La Misión de San Francisco de Asís—the City of San Francisco. He helped to found El Pueblo de Nuestra Señora de Los Angeles del Rio Porciuncula: original name of the City of Los Angeles. His Misión de San Luis Obispo de Tolosa became the City of San Luis Obispo. And La Misión de Santa Clara, around which grew the City of Santa Clara, was also founded by the venerable Father, and lies in today's Silicon Valley, where are found all the implements we've created that have brought us closer to thinking of ourselves as gods.

First of the Seven Sacraments: Baptism. For Catholics, Confirmation is baptism *numero dos*. At what the Catholic Church has deemed the *age of reason*, after instruction in the Holy Faith, a bishop confirms the confirmand. Usually, only a bishop performs this Sacrament, except in some cases, where the power's granted to priests. Fray Junípero Serra, in a Pontifical Brief, obtained a ten-year patent to confirm the neophytes of Alta California.

Confessor Junípero Serra was prelate to Fathers Juan Crespí and Francisco Palou. Catholic priests have as many titles as the universe galaxies. Junípero Serra should additionally be titled Blessed, due to his 20th century beatification. Technically, Blessed Father Fray Junípero Serra would need one more miracle confirmed by the Roman Curia before canonization to sainthood; however, His Holiness, Pope Francis has announced his intention to canonize the blessed father. Blessed to many faithful. Blessed are the Native Californians who protest this anticipated canonization.

I tried to calm myself from my apprehension over this trip into the Georgia mountains by listening to the mixed CD my wife had made for me before she was my wife, back when our love was so new even the case that housed this CD hadn't cracked. Her mix hit every emotion, as all mix CDs ought to, specific as they are for their intended audience, and anything but sentimental for an outsider. Yes, this CD included Journey.

I attended Catechism at Our Lady of Refuge, in Castroville, California, my home parish, part of the Diocese of Monterey, a diocese founded by Blessed Father Fray Junípero Serra. In Catechism we colored in Catholic coloring books, and made for our parents construction paper cards that depicted Mary and Joseph, and the appearance of the Archangel Gabriel before Mary upon the Annunciation. We drew symbols of the Holy Trinity—dove, crucifix, P exed with an X (the chi-rho), the triquetra—and celebrated the sanctity of mother and fatherhood. This instruction prepared me for the second of the Seven Sacraments: Holy Communion.

At my First Communion I wore a tiny shirt and tie, like all the other boys. The girls wore elaborate and frilly white gowns. All of us eight-year-olds marrying the Lord.

At the Lullian University Father Serra zealously sought to be a missionary to what he and other Europeans of the time called *the heathen* of New Spain.

On Father Serra's zeal: our English word comes to us from the Greek ζῆλος: transliterated: *zelos*: used in ecclesiastical Latin to describe one with great enthusiasm and energy for God. Today, a derivation—*zealot*—is still used to describe the faithful, but can carry also a negative connotation, as in *Among the zealots of Islam are suicide bombers*, or, *Christian zealots preach that "God hates fags."* In the case of Father Serra, *monomaniacal* is perhaps a more appropriate modern adjective to combine with zeal: so great was Father Serra's monomaniacal zeal for bringing the Gospel to the Natives of North America, that he was willing—in fact hoping—to die in the process.

I spent every Sunday morning in mass at Our Lady of Refuge. Mom roused me from bed, had me dressed in Sunday clothes, and we rushed off in our attempt to make it on time, the station wagon's tires squealing as she floored us out of our housing development onto Highway 156 heading towards Castroville.

In George Lucas's 1977 film *Star Wars* the ghostly voice of the deceased character Obi-Wan Kenobi (indeed, he vanished, leaving nothing but a monastic-looking robe) encourages his former student Luke Skywalker to *Use the Force.* Immediately following this, in a jump cut, the film's antagonist, Darth Vader, preparing to laser the young starfighter into vapors floating in the Death Star's gravitational pull, exclaims, *The Force is strong in this one.* It appears that Darth Vader regularly talks to himself.

Conversos are Jews forced to Catholicism by the Holy Office of the Inquisition. Though the medieval Church suspected all Jews, even those who might have sincerely converted.

The curious eyes of priests spying a converso's home, noting that no smoke emitted skyward come Sabbaths. The priests condemned conversos as heretics, and forced them into confessions. A parade through the cobbled Palma streets from the Jewish Quarter to the plaza, your fellow Mallorcans tossing curses and molded tomatoes, your arms bound, grape-pelted. The platform seating the bishop and priests, the *alcalde*, and other notables of your city in attendance, four thousand eyes. The post upon which you're bound. The fires lick your toes, your heels, your shins. The pain searing, and your screams unmuffled by the silent rapturous crowd. Finally the pain numbed, and your vision of the blue sky, the smoke, scent of roasting human flesh—yours—your vision darkening, then black. The last sound is the hiss of your own fat flaring in the flames.

Sunday mornings give forth a peculiar light: no matter the season on the seasonless California coast, the sun's rays slant, bathing every coast live oak, every Monterey pine and Monterey cypress, in honey-sweet light. The greens of these trees, of our neighborhood lawns, of the moss clinging to the oaks' branches like thousands of old men's beards, tantalized as they sped past outside the car's windows. Later, after church, would come the bicycle rides along the trails that meandered the greenbelts behind my neighbors' homes, football on backyard lawns, and on the television in the fall. Games: redlight/greenlight, duck-duck-goose, ring around the rosy, and baseball. Though later I would be more critical, more cynical, as a child all of this I maintained as evidence enough of God.

In Father Fray Francisco Palou's *Life and Apostolic Labors of the Venerable Father Junípero Serra* he writes of his learning of Father Serra's desire to set out for North America: the walls of the cell were light gray and bare save for a crucifix fixed to the wall above the father's plain plank cot shoved into a corner. A small stool and a table pushed against another wall; a volume of *The Little Flowers of Saint Francis* lay upon the table. Father Palou confessed to his Prelate his desire to mission the heathen, if only God would give him a companion. Father Serra's eyes squinted; tears dribbled down his pale and sickly face. He grasped Father Palou's shoulders. "I, too, have the desire to leave for America, and I have just now been praying that should it be the will of God, a companion would join me."

Miquel Josep Serra took the name *Junípero* after Saint Juniper, one of the original friars admitted to the order by Saint Francis himself. Young Miquel would have read Saint Juniper's life as it was chronicled in *The Little Flowers of Saint Francis*. Saint Juniper famously cooked a meal of a pig's foot for an ailing brother. He found the pig in a field and chased him, caught him down, severed the foot. The field was pastureland, full of cropped grass, glazing golden in the late sun. The pig's screams flowed like the pig's blood, onto the grass, onto the pig's shit, as the pig's bowels emptied. Juniper's habit pig blood-and-shit-stained, he wiped the blade clean on the field grass. The pig hobbled, three-footed, away. When the pig's owner found the Franciscans cooking the pig's foot, he hollered over the friars' thievery.

Juniper told the farmer the story of his desire to cook his brother a simple meal, and of his desire to be charitable. Juniper's arms flung round the pig's owner, the smell of pig's blood and shit mingling with human body odor. Saint Juniper died in 1258 in Italy.

In my town of Castroville, California, Ford station wagons packed with bodies, with wheel wells and fenders muddied from artichoke field mud, sparked the rear bumper along the asphalt. Some would say, "Castroville's getting to be full of Mexicans." California was once Mexico, and before that Nueva España, and before that filled with natives with— for the most part—mutually unintelligible languages. And Indians and Spaniards became mestizos. And white people still complain that Mexicans are coming into the west.

When Father Serra and Fathers Francisco Palou and Juan Crespí left Mallorca aboard an English merchant vessel, the British captain challenged the friars to interpretations of the Gospels. When the captain disagreed with Father Serra, and the Franciscan corrected the captain by referring to scriptural passages that he'd memorized, the defeated Englishman held a knife to the priest's throat and threatened to send his body overboard for mutiny.

I drove en route for a one-bedroom cabin set off a lonely road from a remote highway in the north Georgia mountains where I'd have no cell phone reception. The cabin came with a mini-fridge, a shower and kitchen sink, a twin bed, a desk upon which I'd perch my computer, and the chair in which I'd sit to write. The windows looked out on a swath of mixed evergreen and deciduous forest that, in the duration of my stay would blend into a kaleidoscopic meld of green and the yellow, orange, and red of fall.

Before my sister's first Communion she was unpleasant to my mother because she wanted to wear a big white gown, like those of her friends, the gowns the Mexican girls wore. Mom insisted that my sister don the simple and white dress that Mom herself slipped into for her Sacrament in the 1950s (i.e., it was not ruffled and poofed, and it cost nothing, and it looked nothing like the dresses the Mexican girls might wear). My sister says that what was most important about the Sacrament was that now she would be able to walk to the foot of the altar, like Mom and Dad, and be able to partake of the host, and this made her feel more grown up. Afterwards, she'd realize the host was a little, light yellow wafer that tasted like cardboard, and the wine was vinegary and burned in her throat.

As part of his university education, Father Serra read *The Lives of the Saints*, developing a love for many of the reverent discussed therein, including Saint Bernardine of Siena, who, after contracting bubonic plague by tending to the sick, survived the disease, prompting his devotion to God, and to the spread of the Gospel. When Bernardine preached, his hearers tossed elaborate dresses, fine boots, bottles of liquor and barrels of beer and wine into the bonfires that raged like hell's flames. Bernardine missioned throughout Italy, using a symbol he devised containing the Holy Name of Jesus surrounded by a burning sun. The College of Cardinals urged the Pope to condemn him for heresy on the grounds of idolatry. Most viciously Bernardine preached against sodomites, whom he shouted, cross in hand, were the cause of the plague. When Bernardine preached against sodomy, his hearers spit and wiped their mouths at the vileness of even the word. Father Serra revered Saint Bernardine, for Bernardine resigned from his vicarship in order to mission throughout Italy, where he preached that the sodomites of Venice should have their arms and legs bound and pulled in opposite directions till the bones cracked and separated and the skin stretched and tore while these penitent screamed for God's mercy.

As a boy I lay in bed unable to sleep, daring myself to think these words: "I do not believe in—" And I could not finish. An almost-sentence mentally uttered—streamed by in my mind. I stopped, said I was sorry, that it wasn't true, that I only wanted to see what would happen. Then I said Our Fathers and Hail Marys until finally I drifted off.

The German wine Blue Nun is arguably the first international wine sales phenomenon, due in part to their "whole meal" campaign that ended anxiety over wine pairings. A famous (to Father Serra, anyway) Blue Nun was Sor María Fernández Coronel y Arana de Jésus de Ágreda. After receiving Holy Communion, Reconciliation, Confirmation, Holy Orders, María fell into bouts of quiet religious ecstasy, kneeled in rapturous prayer for days without food or water. The black shoulders of her shawl attracted dust, as she would not stir, save levitating. María de Ágreda flew through the air, across the Atlantic, and across North America, to Texas and New Mexico, and appeared before the Navajo and Apache. This, Catholics call the miracle of bilocation[1]. And so the nun, like the wine, was an interna-

---

1   "This holy virgin burned with a most ardent love for God and for the salvation of souls. One day, she beheld in a vision all the nations of the world. She saw the greater part of men were deprived of God's

tional phenomenon. Now, in America, Americans readily suck down that cheap swill, Blue Nun.

"Pope" comes from *papa*. The Pope is the elected leader of the College of Cardinals, the bishop of Rome, Head of the College of Bishops, Supreme Pontiff of the Universal Church, Patriarch of the West, Primate of Italy, Archbishop and Metropolitan of the Roman Province, Sovereign of the state of Vatican City, the commander-in-chief of the world's oldest standing army, *Servus servorum Dei*, <u>enter pope's papal name here</u>.

I saw Pope John Paul II in the 1980s when he visited Monterey as part of the beatifying of Father Junípero Serra. My mother and I bundled into Fort Ord at three in the morning. In the dark everyone held neon glow sticks that are not so novel now as they were in then, when I was a boy.

---

grace, and running headlong to everlasting perdition. She saw how the Indians of Mexico put fewer obstacles to the grace of conversion than any other nation who were out of the Catholic Church, and how God, on this account, was ready to show mercy to them. Hence she redoubled her prayers and penances to obtain for them the grace of conversion. God heard her prayers. He commanded her to teach the Catholic religion to those Mexican Indians. From that time, she appeared, by way of bilocation, to the savages, not less than five hundred times, instructing them in all the truths of our holy religion, and performing miracles in confirmation of these truths. When all were converted to the faith, she told them that religious priests would be sent by God to receive them into the Church by baptism. As she had told, so it happened. God, in his mercy, sent to these good Indians several Franciscan fathers, who . . . when they asked the Indians who had instructed them, they were told that a holy virgin appeared among them many times, and taught them the Catholic religion and confirmed it by miracles."—Muller, Michael. *The Catholic Dogma: "Extra Ecclesiam Nullus omnino Salvatur."*

I mean this was 1984. I skipped school. The Pope came to Laguna Seca—where they hold the racecar and motorcycle races—and there, from a hillside covered in California brome, we watched the grand papa cart by along the racetrack at a modest seven miles per hour in his bulletproof glass Popemobile. Afterwards the Pope celebrated High Mass at a makeshift altar and I fell asleep.

From Guy Ritchie's film *Snatch*, between two minutes and three minutes-thirty-four seconds, characters disguised as Orthodox Jews planning to rob a diamond dealer, consort thus:
   Thief # 1: The Septuagenarianist scholars misinterpreted the Hebrew word for *young woman* into the Greek word for *virgin*. It was an easy mistake to make because there was only a subtle difference in the spelling. So, they came up with the prophecy: *Behold, a virgin shall conceive and bear us a son.* You understand it was the *virgin* that caught people's attention. It's not every day a virgin conceives and bears a son.
   And then a couple hundred years or two, the next thing you know, you have the Holy Catholic Church.
   Thief # 2: . . . What are you saying?
   Thief # 1: I'm saying, just 'cause it's written does not make it so. It's not important whether it's fact or fiction.

One of my uncles does not think that my brother and I have actually married, because my sister performed the ceremony for me and my wife, and I performed it for my brother. Because we are not wed by a Catholic priest, in full mass, we have thus not committed to the Sacrament of Holy Matrimony.

When Father Serra landed in Vera Cruz he insisted on walking the 245 miles to Mexico City, to the Apostolic College of San Fernando, from whence he missioned to many natives. On this walk, while encamped along the road, he endured a mosquito bite. The sore from this bite Father Serra suffered his entire life. It seems odd that a mosquito bite would last that long. But the only first-hand account, that of Father Francisco Palou, describes the bite as one from a mosquito. I don't know how many times I've been mosquito bitten, but the bites never lasted much more than a week. Then again, we live in a far more sanitary time than did the Blessed Father. Still, in his later life, Father Palou refers to the wound as an "ulcer". Whatever it was, Father Serra had a hole in his leg that hobbled him while he huffed his way from mission to mission.

Recently, while teaching Orwell's *Nineteen Eighty-four*, I realized that Father Serra likely suffered from a varicose ulcer, similar to Orwell's character, Winston Smith. Due to venous hypertension, blood cannot pump into arteries and instead pools. Venous ulcers usually occur on the legs, and are the most common cause of chronic wounds.

Father Serra referred to California as the "vineyard of the Lord," which is ironic now, considering California's wine industry. But the Blessed Father of course alluded metaphorically to souls. My friend says that he never uses metaphor, and that metaphor is as dumb as rocks. I've read almost all of his writing, and there's hardly a line that's not metaphoric. So when he says that a character's head is shook clean of later days, he means it literally, I suppose— that days somehow dirty this person's head. I don't know about that. It seems more advantageous to have a vineyard of the Lord metaphorically, than for the Lord to have an actual vineyard. I mean, what's the Lord going to do with a vineyard?

My grandfather converted to Catholicism for my grandmother. My father converted for my mother. My grandfather was a devout Catholic. My father, not so much. Flannery O'Connor says that the Catholic novelist may not be in tune with the Church, that Catholicism is part of her blood, that the Catholic novelist might not even attend church. My father sounds a little bit like a Catholic novelist, except he doesn't write novels. The Church was definitely a part of Grandpa's blood. I would say that Catholicism has worked its way into my blood, too, for better or worse.

I'd set for myself this goal: I would write. But not just write—I'd write a book about a seventeenth century Catholic friar and missionary. I was dumb enough to believe that if I couldn't accomplish this while in that mountain cabin, I was a failure.

Father Serra arrived at the College of San Fernando in Mexico City, and in his humility he requested that he be admitted as a novice. When appointed *presidente* of the missions of the Sierra Gorda, Serra's colleagues requested that he not be sent, because they would miss his fervent preaching. Blessed Father Fray Junípero Serra stood in the pulpit, dropped his habit, baring his naked chest, and with a barbed whip he flogged himself, exclaiming aloud his unworthiness in the eyes of God. The blood dripped over his pale skin. A parishioner came forward and hollered, "*I* am a sinner, and not the venerable Father, who is a saint!" And, taking the flog from Father Serra, he whipped himself in front of the congregation until he dropped, near death. The parishioners gathered, tears pooling upon the church's stones, the man, whispering a request only for Blessed Father Fray Junípero Serra. The priest came to the man, performed his last rites, communed with him. It was quiet in the church when the man's last breath left his lungs, a tired sigh. Father Serra refused the position of *presidente* of the missions of the Sierra Gorda, but he left Mexico City all the same to mission the Pame Indians as a common priest.

A contemporary Protestant missionary writes of the Pame Indians of San Luis Potosí of the Sierra Gorda, that there are very few Christians among them, that in a region of near five thousand inhabitants, there are but three Christians. He describes the Catholic Church as containing three idols, the central of which is destroyed, having been struck by lightning. He says, "Isn't that strange?" with obvious irony. He says he wants to bring the Gospel to these Godless people, the Pame.

While walking from village to village missioning Indians, mestizos, and *gente de razon*, Father Serra and Father Fray Francisco Palou found that at nightfall they had come to a river's banks, but could not find the crossing in the dark. A voice called from the opposite shore. The fathers said they were children of God on their way to Mexico. The voice instructed the fathers to follow the river south. The voice called every few seconds, and the fathers called back, and so they did not lose each other and shortly they came to the river's crossing. Once on the other side, the fathers met the young man and thanked him for his charity. The man wore rags and said he farmed the region. He asked the fathers where they were staying the night. When the fathers replied that they had no lodging, the man invited them to his home. There the man—along with his young wife, and their intelligent, generous, and pious boy—offered the fathers a meal, and warm beds. In the morning the fathers offered the man and his family their thanks and blessings, and the priests continued on the road to Mexico. They came upon a muleteer who brought with him stench and flies, and who asked the fathers if they had slept under the stars. When they told the muleteer about the man, his family, and his little house, the muleteer said that they must've been hallucinating, for there was no house for over a hundred miles in any direction. Father Serra concluded to Father Palou, "It must have been Joseph, Mary, and the boy Jesus who appeared and housed us last night. Thanks be to God!"

In Catechism I memorized the Act of Contrition. I don't remember it now, except the beginning: *Forgive me Father for I have sinned* . . . This was in preparation for the Sacrament of Holy Reconciliation, where in a confessional I confessed my sins to Father Scott. Father Scott looked like Jesus, at least in Western cultural representations of Jesus since the middle ages, and if Jesus put on a few pounds. Father Scott was longhaired, redheaded, bearded, chubby, tall. When he left church with the procession of altar servers and Eucharistic ministers, yelling, "Sing a New Song Unto the Lord," he smiled, hands folded, and he gazed over his parishioners, and bounced along. For four months every year he lived among the Sioux in Wyoming, where towards the end of his tenure at Our Lady of Refuge, they inducted him as an honorary member of their tribe.

My cabin was set on a berm in a wash upon a hundred million year-old mountainside. The wash ran down to a creek that drained the valley of its intermittent rains. My cabin's roof was mossed and lichened, just like the large propane tank outside the building, which would heat my water for showers and washing dishes.

Early autumn leaves just starting to turn, a splash of red in the green. My first morning I ran six miles: three miles up a mountain, three back down. Who runs up a mountain? I had no idea the road would take me there.

Father Serra learned Pame, a Chichimec language, among the most difficult to learn in the world. He translated the Catechism into Pame and sung mass to the natives.

On Ash Wednesday Mom pulled me briefly from school, took me to mass, where Father Scott drew the penitential cross across my forehead. My schoolmates and I darted around the playground and the halls, brisking from class to class with these ashy crosses drawn on our faces. Only that night or the next morning would water rinse away the cross, swirling it in a vortex down the shower drain. With Lent came Friday's disgusting tuna sandwiches packed into my brown bag lunch, along with an apple, and cookies. We ate fish for lunch and dinner on Fridays; no steaks or hamburgers, spaghetti or porkchops. Salmon, tuna, cod, and—more than anything—fish sticks. Disgusting, breaded, lined on the baking sheet and torched crispy, sometimes black, the-only-way-to-eat-them-with-any-joy-whatsoever-is-with-gallons-of-ketchup, processed Gorton's Fish Sticks.

Blessed Father Fray Junípero Serra preached to the Pame about the Passion and led processions through the pueblo of Jalpan de Sierra hauling a two hundred-pound rough-hewn cross upon his shoulders. He had a life-sized wooden figure carved and attached with hinges to the cross, in order to depict Jesus' Crucifixion and Deposition. Father Serra and the Pame placed the wooden Christ in a casket and, in another procession, heaved the body back through the village and buried it in a vault. Easter Sunday the risen Christ returned in sight to the Indians and Blessed Father Fray Junípero Serra preached the Risen Lord.

Through Lent Our Lady of Refuge shrouded the crucifix in purple. Yards of purple strung over the arms of various crosses inside and outside the nave. Father Scott's vestments were purple. My tongue, stained from grape-flavored Blow-pops and Now & Laters, was purple. Back then I hated tuna fish, though now it's not so bad I think, especially with Diet Pepsi, for some reason. I don't observe fish-eating Fridays anymore, unless I happen to eat fish on Friday, but now it's coincidental. Lent is forty days and forty nights, and for a kid that's a pretty long time. What I remember about Easter is mostly these cookies that a neighbor, Barbara Something-itch, made once when my family visited her house and the sun that day was how it gets in spring: bright but not too hot. Then there were lilies strung upon the pews, lilies in vases flanking the altar, lilies in vases at the entrance to Our Lady of Refuge. Their stench reeked out into the concrete courtyard where Mom milled about talking to whomever, over to the lined spaces where our station wagon sat waiting to cart me home to school-less Sunday freedom. Sometimes we went to Granny and Grandpa's house and other times they visited us. Mom bought Paas Easter Egg dying kits and I stained my fingers and clothes with the food coloring tablets that I'd dropped into the heated water and stinking vinegar. Easter morning brought a hunt. I quested after the Easter basket, overflowing with fake plastic grass and chocolate eggs and chocolate bunnies, and toys, sometimes plastic airplanes bought by Grandpa, a Pan Am flight engineer. Jelly beans. I was not allowed to eat my candy, though, until after church.

Mallorcans cook with a lot of saffron, a spice that would not have been found in North America. In Jalpan de Sierra, San Luis Potosí, Mexico, the staple edible crops are nopales and maguey. Father Serra instructed the Pames on the temporal government, which was the Church. As well, he instructed the Pames on agriculture, teaching them to use a plow and oxen, to sow beans and corn, to sell the surplus of their harvest, and to buy cloth and make clothing. Father Palou writes that by this teaching Father Serra led the Pames away from their natural inclination towards idleness, and lit the torch of civilization for these heathen. Though, in reality the Pames had been part of the complex Aztec Empire for four hundred years prior to Conquistador arrival.

Before I came to Dillard, Georgia, the little mountain town closest to my retreat, I stopped at a grocery store and loaded up with the requisite foodstuffs: steaks and chicken, cereal, milk and coffee, bread and sandwich meat, and vegetables. But I'd also packed with me, perhaps naively, knowing what kind of a drinker I can be, and without realizing the depths to which I'd eventually fall: a twelve pack of Pabst Blue Ribbon beer.

When I finally fulfilled the Sacrament of Holy Reconciliation, I recited for Father Scott my sins. I lied. I beat up my sister. I stole a toy from my brother. I did not confess to Father Scott all of my sins. I thought about sex. I lied. I touched a girl's butt at school. I lied. In fact, I am a tremendous liar. There are some things you cannot tell a priest.

Mallorcans greet one another, "¡Amar a Dios!" Father Serra took this expression to North America and saluted the Natives, and there, in Upper California, the salutation became common during the colonial era.

We left for mass early on Easter, with Granny and Grandpa there to keep Mom from her dallying that always made us late. We all knew what mass on Easter Sunday would bring: droves of people, some of them the parishioners we saw every other Sunday of the year, but most were folks I didn't recognize. Where did they all come from? Castroville is a small town (a little more than five or six thousand), but on Easter Sunday Our Lady of Refuge about burst (or at St. Helena Catholic Church, when we went to Granny and Grandpa's). People lined the walls under the Stations of the Cross and the stained glass windows. They stood four-deep at the back, in front of the closed confessional booths, and spilled into the narthex. The church opened the usually unused choir loft and those pews also filled, high above the floor and the altar where Father Scott's arms raised as he blessed the Sacrament.

Upon finishing his missionary work in the Sierra Gorda Father Serra returned to the College of San Fernando. He missioned throughout the countryside surrounding Mexico City. In Antequera he encountered Pie de la Soledad, a young woman living in sin with a married man, Martín Guzman. Martín had left his wife in Spain and had come to Mexico, where he met Pie de la Soledad, a mestiza. She had lain with Martín now for fourteen years. Father Serra learned all this through the confession of Pie de la Soledad. Serra urged Pie de la Soledad to leave Martín, and move into her own house, which she did. But Martín pleaded with her to come home. He said, *Yo te quiero, necesito tu soledad, Soledad.* He chanted to her window and held a torch. Pie de la Soledad asked Father Serra for help, so that she would not again fall into the sin in which she had lived for so long with Martín Guzman, for before the arrival of Blessed Father Fray Junípero Serra, the Church had been absent from Antequera, and sin spread rampant. Now Pie de la Soledad knew that she would go to heaven, because she had confessed her sins. Father Serra arranged for Pie de la Soledad to move in with María Gonzales, a prominent old woman in Antequera, a woman of virtue and chastity, and she— Father Serra promised—would protect Pie de la Soledad from Martín Guzman. But Martín Guzman chanted to the window of the house of María Gonzales: *¡Me rompas el corazon! ¡Me muero, me muero! ¡Moriré sin tu amor!* But María Gonzales would not allow Pie de la Soledad to respond to his urgings. She put a rosary into Pie de la Soledad's fist, and sat her on the cot in the candlelight, and together they recited the Hail Mary, the Our Father, the Apostle's Creed, Glory to God the Father. The planet shook. Ruptured and shifting continental plates. Pottery shattered on the earthen floor. Outside, hanging from the gate in front of the house: Martín Guzman's swinging corpse. Pie de la Soledad sheared her hair, donned sackcloth, and barefooted the refuse-strewn streets of Antequera, confessing her sins before everyone, begging God's forgiveness, and because of Pie de la Soledad and the doomed fate of Martín Guzman, many feared God, and Blessed Father Fray Junípero Serra reaped much fruit for the Lord.

Beyond anecdotes like the above (about which I have taken certain liberties: in the history, the woman and her lover and the woman with whom the girl took refuge all go unnamed, for example), little is known about Father Serra and his life between 1758 and 1768. Father Palou is curiously silent about these years. During these years Father Serra worked as comisario for the Holy Office of the Inquisition of New Spain. Perhaps Father Palou realized that the Inquisition would be looked upon unfavorably, and in the efforts of eventual canonization left such details out of the *Historical Account of the Life and Apostolic Labors of the Venerable Father Fray Junípero Serra and of the Missions which He Founded in Northern California and the New Establishments of Monterey.*

Another such anecdote dates to 1766 in Valle del Maiz, Mexico. Dominga de Jesús charged María Pasquala with witchcraft, claiming Pasquala was killing her with evil spells. Father Serra interrogated María Pasquala in the tiny stone cell ubiquitous around Franciscans, and into which María Pasquala had been imprisoned. In the gloom of said cell, Father Serra asked of María Pasquala, "*¿Conoces Dominga de Jesús?*", the Dominga de Jesús who suffered from a cough and went to María Pasquala for a remedy, no differently than today, should one visit a herbalist, a practitioner of homeopathy. María Pasquala prepared a concoction for

Dominga de Jesús that seemed to alleviate Dominga de Jesús's cough, but within a week her head ached and her fingers swelled, then the cough returned with such violence that blood stained the cloth when she phlegmed. Fearing death, Dominga de Jesús went to Father Antonio. The secular lieutenant secured an unnotarized "confession" from María Pasquala, a confession worthless in a court of law. Father Serra said to María Pasquala: "If you do not confess that you have made a pact with the devil. And that you have performed spells intended to destroy Dominga de Jesús, you will be charged with perjury." He cited her invalid confession.

The "confession" of María Pasquala:

"[María Pasquala] declared that she made a pact with *el Demonio* a year ago, and that the Devil had tricked her, and he had won her soul, and that she was content. She said this devil was known as the Devil who carries the pall [*el Diablo que cargaba el Balleton*]. This devil used to go by her side, and he told her to gather herbs to do harm to the *Cristianos*; and that she had killed with these herbs a man as the Devil had commanded . . . and that the Devil had commanded her to poison Dominga de Jesús because she was a good singer. . . and had told her to make a little doll of rags [*muñeca de trapos*] . . . and that she brought *el Balleton* meat and candies, . . . and that he got mad at her when she mentioned God, . . . and that when she went out she sometimes came upon him in the form of a Pame Indian, a coyote, a cat, or a skunk, . . . and that he embraced her when he was in the form of a Pame Indian, and that she slept with him and that they had carnal relations when he came to her, . . . and that at night the Devil took her to where there were bats . . . and that in the form of bats some of their accomplices came to suck the blood of little children, and that she had sucked the blood of little ones who died without baptism, . . . and that some of the Pame Indians had brought Peyote and that others had gathered at the mission of Valle del Maiz, all of them widows, and that they too came as bats, and that they too had their little Devils and that they too sucked blood from little ones . . . and that *el Balleton* had told her to get a bone from a dead person in a cemetery so that they could have good luck in their gambling, . . . and that *el Balleton* had told her to stop praying the Rosary and to not pay attention to the saints and that when she went to confess that she should not confess more than two sins, and that that was enough, and that when she took Communion she should take the Eucharist from her mouth, place it on her finger, and stick it to a beam beneath the *Comulgatorio* . . . and that she should not pray . . . and that when she asked the Devil where he went, he said he went to Hell or to the caves and that he got mad at her for not wanting to go with him."[2]

Because Father Serra had little to no interaction with the opposite sex, and because she was a widow and of mixed race, it's likely he felt uncomfortable around María Pasquala.

This is the prayer we chanted, holding hands, every night before dinner: Bless us oh Lord, for these our gifts, which we are about to receive, our bounty through Christ, our Lord, Amen. Then we all said, God bless the cook! When we were with my grandparents, Grandpa said, God bless Chicky, and Holly, and Harvey, and Boots—all the dead dogs.

2   From *Junípero Serra: California's Founding Father* by Steven Hackel

Blessed Father Fray Junípero Serra's Alta California vineyard of the Lord. My Grandma and Grandpa owned a vineyard in the Napa Valley. Father Serra likely never saw the Napa Valley, as the Spanish had not explored that far north during his lifetime.

After mass the church held an Easter egg hunt for the children and, given baskets, we hopped about like rather large bunnies—me in a little short-pant suit, and later in slacks and sport jacket, fit for a boy on Easter—spying eggs disguised beneath granite slabs hauled up from the bed of the Napa River and now holding flowerbeds, or in the fork of the cottonwood in Granny and Grandpa's backyard from where at twilight the bats flit out in a whorl, snatching mosquitoes that tried to retreat with the spring day going down to cool night. Eggs hidden in the dish of the church water fountain on the side of the building, the same water fountain we'd run to drink from in the middle of our marbles games during Catechism, or after baseball practice at the ballpark that sat across the street.

In 1767 Charles II expelled the Jesuits because of their perceived political influence, and the missions of Baja California would be abandoned, but the College of San Fernando, that reverent Apostolic bevy of Franciscan Friars, stepped in to fill the void. Thus Blessed Father Fray Junípero Serra would get one step closer to attaining his ultimate goal of missioning the un-Europeanized natives (his "heathen") of North America. Earlier he nearly had his chance to achieve this goal, with the Apaches of New Mexico and Texas, where he was initially assigned. But, because of violent revolts (friars' brains clubbed, missions charred to ash) that resulted from the Franciscans' original attempts at establishing missions, the Church fell back on this assignment.

Around the fifth or sixth grade we learned about the California missions, and my classmates and I built model missions. I read that the Indians and Spaniards made adobe bricks to build their missions, so I made miniature adobes. I built cardboard forms and lined shoeboxes with them. From my backyard I unearthed earth and mixed it with the California brome that my father had weed-whacked, comingling with water, and I made my adobe mix. Into the shoeboxes this mix went, to dry in the sun. Sunlight was rare, with our foggy central coast weather, and a hairdryer came in handy, a device of which Spaniards and Indians alike were devoid. Once dried, I stacked my tiny bricks and formed up walls then tiled a roof. I whitewashed said walls with a watercolor paintbrush and plaster of paris. My mission. I had no Indians because by the time I was born almost all of the Indians were dead.

When Father Serra left for the missions of Baja California, he embarked for the port of San Blas in Nyarit, from whence he sailed to Loreto, Baja California, and from there he traveled by foot to the northern missions.

This just came in my email inbox, from my uncle:

SIPPING VODKA

A new priest at his first mass was so nervous he could hardly speak. After mass he asked the monsignor how he had done. The monsignor replied, "When I'm worried about getting nervous at mass, I put a glass of vodka next to the water pitcher. If I get nervous, I take a sip." Next Sunday he took the monsignor's advice. At the beginning of the homily, he got nervous and took a drink. He proceeded to talk up a storm. Upon his return to his office after the mass, he found the following note on the door:

1. Sip the vodka, don't shoot it.

2. There are 10 Commandments, not 12.

3. There are 12 disciples, not 10.

4. Jesus was consecrated, not constipated.

5. Jacob wagered his donkey, he did not bet his ass.

6. We do not refer to Jesus Christ as the late J.C.

7. The Father, Son, and Holy Spirit are not referred to as Daddy, Junior, and The Spooky.

8. David slew Goliath, he did not kick the shit out of him.

9. When David was hit by a rock and was knocked off his donkey, don't say he was stoned off his ass.

10. We do not refer to the cross as the "Big T."

11. When Jesus broke the bread at the last supper he said, "Take this and eat it for it is my body." He did not say "Eat me."

12. The Virgin Mary is not called "'Mary with the Cherry."

13. The recommended grace before a meal is not "Rub-A-Dub-Dub thanks for the grub, Yeah God."

While I sat there in my little cabin, trying to write, I watched a beetle attempting to crawl up the venetian blinds. But he could not gain a foothold on the plastic, and so climbed upon the twine that held the blinds together, and from blind-to-blind his little legs scrabbled. He was almost at the top, but he turned south yet again, Sisyphean in his efforts.

My mountain retreat proved homey, if isolated. Before meeting my wife I'd been alone with no one but my cat and my few friends. But this was a different kind of solitude. After my first evening and night I situated my suitcase and packed away my clothing in the spare pine dresser next to the bed, and atop which sat a telephone that did not work. I set up the bathroom with my towel and soap and shampoo and deodorant, my toothbrush and paste. I loaded my food into the refrigerator and in front of it all, still packaged in its cardboard box I loaded my twelve pack of beer. I sat at the table where I would write and stared out the window at the view that would become so familiar as I watched the subtle changes of the seasons transpire in this forest. I stared at my computer's blank screen. I'd internalized the year's research: Junípero Serra's life from his childhood in Mallorca to his schooling at the Lullian University to his embarking for North America and his eventual landing in California. I'd recorded what seemed to me important facts about syphilis, about death rates of Native Californians, about the influx of Spaniards and other European-descended migrants, about the rates of mission growth, and also their decline. This information jumbled in my mind. I couldn't find a place on which to land. How was I to render all of this information into a novel? I cracked open *Wittgenstein's Mistress* and read paragraph after paragraph, and after a while I opened a beer. Then another beer, and then another.

There are so many J's here, at this colony: Jamie (me); Jamie (the colony director); Janey (a fellow artist); Jenny (a fellow artist); Jennifer (a fellow artist). Junípero. Jesus.

I was doing fine I had a panic attack.

After serving as *Presidente* of the Baja California missions for a year after the Jesuits' expulsion, Blessed Father Fray Junípero Serra and Visitador-General José de Gálvez planned to found three missions in Alta California: the first in the port of San Diego, the second at the port of Monterey, and a third, San Buenaventura, between the other two, as they were separated by a distance of over four hundred miles.

Easter dinner Mom roasted a leg of lamb and served it with mint jelly. I still cannot stand mint jelly, but I've come around to lamb. Lamb of God. Take away the sins of the Earth. Lamb of God, fatty on my tongue. Lamb of God, dressed with mashed potatoes and steamed broccoli. Then came ordinary time, which is not what I would have called it then, for everything was ordinary as a Catholic boy: "something regular, customary, or usual. Ecclesiastical: an order or form for divine service, especially that for saying Mass; the service of the Mass exclusive of the canon. History/Historical: a member of the clergy appointed to prepare condemned prisoners for death."

Under first century Judaic law, calling oneself a Messiah—or a king—would not have been heretical[3], and nonetheless would not have been punished by crucifixion. Crucifixion, as a punishment via the Roman Empire, would have been reserved for insurrectionists against the state[4]. Jerusalem would have seen upwards of 400,000 Jewish pilgrims during Passover[5], and extra soldiers were brought to the city from the coast to enforce peace. The historical Jesus is sometimes theorized to have preached an apocalyptic ministry[6], the coming of the Kingdom of Heaven, and the rise of a Jewish state. Thus, Jesus bears his cross, upon which he will be crucified, to Calvary. The cross is rough-hewn and large. It looks very heavy. Jesus has already been flogged, and the crown of thorns forces blood streams down his forehead and back. In those rivers of blood are rivers of blood and in those rivers tiny fish swim upriver, to their spawning ground, inside the man, inside his heart, and there the fish give birth to guppies that drown in the blood river, their parents feeding microscopic grizzlies. Should there have been a historical crucifixion, Jesus did not likely carry an entire cross, but the gibbet that would affix to the permanent palus drilled into stony ground. Still, the gibbet could have easily weighed as much as the man carrying it.

---

3   http://en.wikipedia.org/wiki/Pharisees

4   Oldfather, William A. "Livy I.26 and the Supplicium de More Maiorum." Transactions of the American Philological Association 39 (1908), 4972. http://penelope.uchicago.edu/Thayer/E/Journals/TAPA/39/Supplicium_de_More_Maiorum*.html#note52

5   Sanders, E. P. *The Historical Figure of Jesus*. New York: Penguin, 1993. 249.

6   Ibid. Ch. 15.

Visitador-General José de Gálvez was so impressed and moved to action by Father Serra's zeal to work in the vineyard of the Lord, that he personally oversaw the repairs of the vessels that would carry the *presidente* and his fellow Franciscans north from Loreto to San Diego. The *San Carlos* and the *San Antonio* both needed recaulking, and, lacking caulking materials, the Visitador-General himself showed his workmen how to extract and use the gum of the pitayo cactus. José de Gálvez worked like a commoner to help get Father Serra's vessel ready, so says Father Palou, for working like a commoner, when one's a nobleman, is virtuous.

Grandpa always said, *Shape up, or ship out.*

The second ship, the *San Antonio*, became stranded in what would later become Cabo San Lucas due to contrary winds. I don't think there was much at Cabo San Lucas at this time: cactus, rock, sand. No Cabo Wabo, no Planet Hollywood. I have bad memories of Cabo San Lucas. I have done very stupid things there. At least it disturbs me when I think about them. More on that when we come to it, that godless moment in my life.

The Spanish Crown, under Carlos II, worried that the Russians threatened to advance on land that Spain had already claimed as Alta California. The Crown could not spare soldiers in occupying forts that did not exist up the California coast. But they did have Franciscan friars. The Franciscans absolutely believed that the Spanish crown wanted to occupy California for the sole purpose of bringing Christ to the pagans, to win souls for God.[7]

---

7   "It is usually stated that the Spanish court at Madrid received

In 1769, in California, Father Serra founded Mission San Diego de Alcalá, named for Saint Didacus. Didacus spent his last years at the Convento de Santa María de Jésus de Alcalá, where he died from a fragrant abscess: this puss-draining hole in his body emitted a pleasant smell. When Henry IV of Spain broke his arm while hunting, after praying to Saint Didacus he had the saint's body removed from its casket so that the king might touch the corpse. Upon doing so, the King's arm was healed. In another Didacus story, the Prince of Asturias after fornicating and reveling all night, suffered a dramatic fall and gave himself a concussion. The next morning, he was partially paralyzed, blind in one eye, and the pain and swelling in his head had become unbearable. Still able to talk, he asked for the intervention of Saint Didacus. The Saint was brought beside the prince's deathbed, and the prince's hand laid upon the one-hundred-year-old uncorrupted corpse. When the prince awakened from a long sleep, he said that Didacus had come to him in a dream, assuring him that he would not die, and he did not, at least not then.

As it was in California when Blessed Father Fray Junípero Serra served as *presidente* of the missions, so it is in Vatican City today: the Church is the State. Today, the Catholic

reports about Russian aggressions in the Pacific northwest, and sent orders to meet them by the occupation of Alta California, wherefore the expeditions of 1769 were made. This view contains only a smattering of the truth. It is evident from [José de] Gálvez's correspondence of 1768 that he and [Carlos Francisco de] Croix had discussed the advisability of an immediate expedition to Monterey, long before any word came from Spain about the Russian activities." From Chapman, Charles E. *A History of California: The Spanish Period.* New York: The MacMillan Company, 1921.

Church and the Vatican City operate under the oldest form of law still in use.

Charles III of Spain ordered José de Gálvez, prior to engaging the Franciscans in the colonization of Alta California: "Occupy and fortify San Diego and Monterey for God and the King of Spain."

I've had two panic attacks that I know of, with this being the second. They're hard to describe: I feel as if I've drunk too much coffee. My heart throbs in my chest. I'm agitated, anxious, and restless. A tingling sensation runs up the left side of my body. I feel small but sharp pains in my chest, on my left side. These feelings make me fear I'm having a heart attack, and the panic I'm already enduring exacerbates. The problem with my panic attacks is multifold: most people who suffer from these report the attacks lasting from fifteen minutes to a few hours. So far, of my two panic attacks, with this one while in the mountains being the shortest, mine last a minimum of three days. I cannot sleep when I have these attacks, and when I doze I suffer from night terrors. But what scares me most, I think, is that there are only two things that make me feel better: running for miles and miles and miles, and drinking. The running makes me forget about the feelings I'm experiencing and I sweat out a bunch of energy. The drinking helps put me at ease and lets me sleep. But this I know is not healthy behavior.

By my third day in my cabin I'd driven back to the nearby town of Clayton where I'd stocked up on coffee and food, but I also purchased a case of beer, a few bottles of white and red wine, and, stopping by a package store, I bought liquor. In doing so I succumbed to what I told myself was self-medication. But the real low point came the night before, when I'd run out of beer at around 11:30 PM and, unable to sleep, I dressed, started the Toyota, and drove to the nearest gas station in Dillard. By the time I'd reached the gas station it was midnight and I probably smelled of all the beer I'd drunk, as the middle-aged, bearded, and check-shirted clerk (like something out of a movie set in the rural South) gave me a sidelong look then glanced at the clock and said, "You just missed it."

"Just missed it?"

"Can't sell you any alcohol, son, not after midnight."

I don't know if this was true, that they had some county ordinance that prevented early-morning alcohol sales (likely), or if the clerk thought that I certainly didn't need any more beer and wouldn't sell me any (possibly). Either way, I simply turned on my heels, returned to my car, and drove back to my cabin. I didn't even bother to return the beer to the cooler from where I'd selected it. I did not say, "Oh, darn. Thanks anyway." I sat in my cabin and stared again at my computer while my leg went all jumpy from the panic, and in this way I spent a sleepless night.

In last night's terrors my father yelled my name, seeming to stand right beside the bed, "Jamie!" Keys inserted and jiggled in the door's lock. Footsteps stepped to the bed, the back of my side-turned body. I felt a body's weight pressed against mine. Another rushed expulsion. I lay sweating, screaming, heart charging. I get strange inside-the-brain feelings that I cannot describe except that it feels like the inside of my head is falling, or caving in, and everywhere else, the rest of my body, feels nothing at all.

Due to the ships' delays, Father Serra traveled on foot from Loreto to San Diego, stopping along the way to see his friend Father Palou. Palou writes of Serra, that his wounded leg and foot—from the insect bite, many years before, a wound that would ail Serra for the rest of his life—caused Father Palou to weep for his beloved friend. These brothers worked close together through most of their lives, even when separated by hundreds of miles. They remained close in one another's heart. When they saw each other again, an embrace, confessions of sins, touching of hands, fingers across faces. Shame surged through their bodies. When Junípero Serra founded the mission at San Diego he was fifty-six years old.

At the moment that I write this, Junípero Serra founded the first mission in Alta California 227 years after Juan Rodriguez Cabrillo first sailed along its coast and Europeans discovered the territory. That would be like if Independence Hall was abandoned after the signing of the American Declaration of Independence, until today, 239 years later.

The Kumeyaay Indians of northern Baja and Southern Alta California—in the area of San Diego Bay—first encountered Europeans on September 28, 1542. Most of the natives ran away, frightened (smart?) at the sight of the strange people and their boat. Those who remained communicated through signs that news had come to the coast from inland that other men like the Spaniards who landed by sea had already reached them. When Juan Rodriguez Cabrillo's men remained onshore for fishing, within time the Kumeyaay began shooting arrows at the intruders.

In Juan Rodriguez Cabrillo's diary, he writes that he landed on the California coast in the Santa Barbara Channel and met Pimugnan Indians. A señora, chieftain of many pueblos in the Pimugnans' matriarchal culture, stayed aboard Cabrillo's ship for three nights. Through signs, the Spaniards learned from her that in the land's interior there were many more pueblos and much maize. The native woman had heard reports of other bearded and cloth-clad men, likely from Hernando de Alarcón's expedition up the Colorado River Delta. These "heathen" offered Cabrillo and his men their tamales, which the Spaniards called "a good food." These same people, the Blessed Father Fray Junípero Serra would later call gentiles, lazy, uncivilized, to whom he brought God, measles, syphilis, guns, and coarse cloth. The Pimugnans brought to Cabrillo fresh water, fish, and wood. In return the Spanish Captain gave to them clay beads. In 1992 the United States Postal Service issued a twenty-nine cent stamp in honor of Juan Rodriguez Cabrillo.

A portion of California Highway One is called the Cabrillo Highway, and it runs between Santa Cruz and Watsonville. A girl I met at school in my sophomore year of college turned out to be from the Santa Cruz Mountains, near my hometown on the shores of the Monterey Bay, and I offered this girl a ride home for winter break. First we stopped at my family's cabin in Squaw Valley, in the Sierra Nevada Mountains, where we curled together on the floor in front of the fireplace, watching *South Park*. I was too shy to do much more than kiss her. After a week back home, with her calling me, and me making mad dashes past the redwoods up Cabrillo Highway from Monterey to the Santa Cruz Mountains, we found ourselves at my parents' home surrounded by oaks while my folks were out of town. There we stripped naked and touched each other the way naked people do. We could have been native Californians, and in a sense we were. Another night later, when I kissed her, she said, We should really stop. I said, What's wrong? The fog was thick. She said, I've gotten used to kissing you, and I have a boyfriend, you know. This was, as they say, news to me. The house got too hot. When that boyfriend called, that very night, and she turned away from me, her ear to the phone, I snuck out of that sweaty house and rushed Cabrillo Highway all the way home at ninety plus. I haven't been in the Santa Cruz Mountains since.

When Father Junípero, Portolá, and the accompanying fathers and soldiers first encountered the natives of southern California, these were Indians who spoke the Tipai, Ipai, and Kumeyaay languages of the Yuman family of the Hokan stock. As Father Serra considered the Indians of the region as related to his mission, these people came to be known erroneously as Diegueños.

Traveling north overland up Baja California, Captain Don Gaspar de Portolá, Blessed Father Fray Junípero Serra, and *soldados de cuera*, came to what would be called El Valle de Los Christianos, for here the venerable father baptized the first of the virgin heathen he would encounter on his sojourn to Alta California. Later, at the Missions, baptized Indians (called neophytes) were forcibly kept on mission grounds and in native rancherias that the padres called *reducciones*.

Father Serra saw the two huddled beyond the trees and ordered the leatherjackets to catch them down. One Indian, after the long chase—during which his companion launched himself from the cliff into the sea, and the second lay prone upon the ground and was forced, after many blows to the head, to his knees—submitted to the Lord Jesus. Blessed Father Fray Junípero Serra, raising a cross to God, fingers pressed to the Indian's forehead, chanted: *Ego te baptizo in nomine Patris, et Filii, et Spiritus Sancti.* He prayed for the heathen's conversion, while the savage shuddered like a wet dog. Father Serra's utterances to the sky and that native huddled to the ground, a leatherjacket's musket-barrel cold against his head skin. The man aching, his muscles swelling.

Soldados de cueras (Leatherjacket Soldiers) *reglamentos* armed the frontiersmen with the Spanish M 1757 musket and a miquelet pistol, both ball-loading firearms. They also carried an *espada*, a long, trident-tipped lance, and a purple shield bearing the royal Spanish crest, and a *puñal*, a dagger. They wore their namesake jackets, which were more of a knee-length vest-like piece of armor, and made from three plies of deerskin that native arrows and spears could not pierce. They donned the *Texcuco*, a wide-brimmed hat, with turned-up edges, and buckskin leggings that protected their shins to the knee. A company was called a *caballería*, and while most men in the *caballería* lacked some of their arms or ammo or both, they out-armed and out-armored the Native Californians who mostly went about nude, and whose weapons were technologically inferior to the loud and deadly guns that the *soldados* needed to fire but once to induce terror.

My sister tells me that she sits next to a handsome man on a flight across the country. After chitchat, she withdraws her book. She's reading Kevin Sampsell's *A Common Pornography*. After a few moments, the handsome man also reads from his book—his leather-bound Bible. Sister thinks, *too bad*, for she's not interested in religious zealots. She falls asleep. Later, settled in Nashville, she opens her volume and out falls a Jesus-covered card that reads, *You can still find God and Salvation!* Because that handsome God-fearing young man saw that word—*pornography*.

Having come to the valley of Vellicata, Father Serra founded a new mission, to link San Diego to the missions of old California. Vellicata would cut that distance between San Diego and the next mission, San Francisco de Borja (more than 180 miles over waterless land), in half. In Vellicata the fathers discovered many heathen, the first virgin Indians the friar would meet. He describes the encounter: he was astonished, that he had only read about it, but it was true: the men were naked as Adam, and showed no shame at their nakedness. Father Serra made gifts to the natives of dried figs and tobacco. The Indians in turn gifted fish that the Spaniards' cook deemed inedible. Father Serra told the Indians through hand signs to come and visit the mission and Father Fermín Lasuén, who would be left in charge of Mission San Fernando de Vellicata. He encouraged them to bring as many of their friends and relatives as possible.

Much of the history concerning Father Serra has considered the Franciscans to have good intentions, and that the natives of the Californias were in desperate need of God and "civilization." Msgr. Francis J. Weber, in his truncated compendium of Maynard J. Geiger's *The Life and Times of Fray Junípero Serra*, refers to Indian medicine men as "wizards" who practiced a barbaric remedy of sucking at the affected body parts of the ill or wounded, and withdrawing from their mouths stones or organic matter, claiming to have extracted the evil ailment.

In the third Station of the Cross, when Jesus falls the first time, he drops to a knee, or lays prone, or supports himself on an elbow. The cross angles over his shoulder, defying physics. Among the last of miracles, the cross does not teeter or tip to one side, does not crush the man below. Soldiers, snapping whips, leer. Other soldiers wield staffs, clubs, or the blunt ends of spears with which they jab and prod the man like a cow. These men, already charged with an unhappy task, want this to end as soon as possible, and so get back to guarding the temple, the Roman state house, returning home to a loving wife, a daughter, meat steaming on the table, the games that weekend.

At first I noticed only that when I had an erection, it felt good. It was some time before I realized that touching it made it feel even better. I never had any guilt about this. In fact, when I was a boy, it was funny to get an erection, because I didn't quite know what was happening. My mother would see it through my pants or underwear and laugh and say something like, "Put your little boner away" as if it was something I could produce and hide through sheer will.

The character of Quint in the Steven Spielberg film *Jaws* is Ahabesque, monomaniacally on a quest to kill a great white shark. He grows so intent on killing the shark that he puts his and his shipmates' lives at risk, burning out the ship's engine, setting the *Orca* adrift in the Atlantic while hounded by a twenty-five-foot-long fish. Eventually, the shark attacks the boat, catching Quint in its jaws while Quint struggles and stabs at the shark with a machete, only to be dragged off the boat, underwater. A spreading blood cloud.

Father Serra's sore from the insect bite in Mexico that still plagued him caused leg pain and made walking difficult. Nevertheless, he insisted on travelling from Mission San Fernando de Vellicata to the port of San Diego on foot. When the pain became unbearable Governor Portolá ordered that a chaise be constructed from the small trees and shrubs that grew in the vicinity, and upon this chaise, the converted Indians from Baja California who were forced to accompany the expedition north were to carry Father Serra to San Diego. But Blessed Father Fray Junípero Serra instead prayed to God, and he went to a muleteer and asked for him to apply a remedy to his sore. The muleteer laughed, said that he knew nothing about such matters, that he knew only how to care for his mules. So Father Serra asked the muleteer to treat him as one of his mules, one with a sore on its leg, and apply to the mule's problem in the same fashion. The muleteer, Juan Antonio Coronel, took some tallow and herbs from the fields, crushed the solution together and heated it over a fire. When the solution was soft enough, he applied it atop Father Serra's sore. That night the Blessed Father slept well, and he awakened much revived, a mule of God able again to walk to San Diego.

Of the California natives with whom the missionaries came into contact, there were up to thirty-nine different languages or dialects. Yet they shared their misunderstanding of Spaniards' devotion to abstract notions. For a California Indian, all members of one's community at some point prepare to journey for the world beyond. For Christians, the afterlife is divided: some go to Heaven, some to Hell.

Were I to imagine how the native Californians thought of the Spaniards, with my white person's limited understanding and stereotyping, it might sound something like this: "The ones who came with the strange beasts that grunt and shit along the trail, those who wear the bark upon their chests and legs, and carry the sticks that make thunder, they have with them the power men. The power men wear grey capes and carry sticks that talk to the gods. They plant these sticks in the ground. From there the sticks require gifts. So the Indians bring the sticks and the power men gifts, and seek to learn. But the men who wear the bark and carry the sticks that make thunder are bad men. They chase the women into the chaparral, and let their grunting shitting animals into the fields to eat the food. When the Indian chases the beasts away the men get angry and make fire with their thunder sticks, fire that kills."

I was baptized by Father Jim, who had dark hair, a dark beard, and black-rimmed glasses. Father Jim also baptized my sister, but after that he left Our Lady of Refuge for another parish. Not long after that he left the priesthood. When I was in college in Reno, Nevada, (Father) Jim also was at college in Reno, earning a PhD. in I-don't-remember-what. I suppose the dark hair, beard, and glasses made me think doctorally of him. He called me one day when I was in the midst of a breakup, after I'd twice attempted suicide, and my mother was desperate for me to get help. She must've phoned him, somehow finding his number.

And Jim, years now out of Our Lady of Refuge's parish, twenty years since my baptism, years even since he'd left the priesthood and the Catholic faith, still made the effort to bring me back in. At the time, though, I didn't respond. More shocked than anything to hear his voice, I said, How are you Father Jim? Then, I guess I shouldn't call you 'Father.' He said it was okay, just call him Jim. When he asked if I wanted to talk I said, Not really. He said, Call your mother; she's worried about you.

Upon the founding of Mission San Diego, Father Serra, his fellow padres, the soldiers, and remaining sailors that had survived into the port, struggled to live. Everyone was dying of scurvy. The packet boats *San Carlos* and *San Antonio* sat at anchor. The crew of the *San Carlos*, save the cook, was decimated. A third boat, the *San Jose*, was never again seen after leaving San Blas. The pagans came to the Spaniards, curious, and hefting with them their war weapons: bows and arrows, and clubs. The padres offered the Indians food, which the Indians would not accept. The Natives thought the food must be what caused the illness rampaging through the camp. Soon, the Indians became bold and stole what interested them: clothing. They ripped away the blankets of the sick and dying. They even paddled out to the *San Carlos* to cut away the ship's sails, until the sole soldier remaining at guard onboard fired the ship's cannon, scattering the frightened Californians. The Indians attacked the Spaniards on land. Father Serra remained inside the little wooden chapel which had been built to celebrate mass, and he prayed that all lives be spared, especially the Indians', for he wished that they would not die without being baptized.

If you've ever been to San Diego or Baja California, you'd be surprised that these Spanish expeditions, and the Kumeyaay and other natives who inhabited these environs, survived at all. The land appears barren, covered with sparse brush, without trees, and little water. It is especially surprising that the Spaniards managed to survive. While the Indians knew that there were edible agave and sotol plants, along with cactus, snakes, lizards, mice, desert fox, and coyotes to hunt, and fish, mollusks, and crustaceans to catch in the sea, the "civilized" Spaniards would have looked at the land as "unimproved," and were completely unprepared for survival.

As a Boy Scout I learned wilderness survival at Camp Pico Blanco, in the mountains of Big Sur, where two hundred years ago the Esselen lived and were missioned by Father Fermín Lasuén, successor to Father Serra as *presidente* of the missions of Alta California. The Esselen would barely survive missionization. There are fewer than a thousand alive today, and none of them lays claim to their original territory in the Santa Lucia Mountains. At Camp Pico Blanco I learned to use a green branch of pine to clean the teeth and mouth, and for vitamin C, for the pinesap contains this, along with acids that naturally refresh the mouth. I learned to build a shelter against a fallen log, to cover the shelter with green boughs thick enough to repel rain. The camp leaders came in the night and tested the sturdiness of our shelter by hopping atop and pouring a canteen upon it, to test its weatherproofness. This is what happens in the land of the Esselen today.

I was once fearless and prepared in the wilderness. In survival training, they led us blindfolded to a California mountaintop. They allowed, carried with us, all that we could on our person, without a pack of any sort. We built survival kits that fit onto our belts or in a pocket. They removed our blindfolds, said, *See you in the morning*. I was eleven years old, but never scared through that training. Yesterday I went for a hike, wary of bears, since I'd seen them in the area. I suppose my fear was due to the locals here in these Georgia mountains talking about a bear overpopulation. I know better. To scare a bear, stand straight up and wave your arms and yell. If you can use anything to make loud noises, do so. Whatever you do, don't run. While jogging I worried that a bear might want to eat me since I was running—à la prey to the predator—away.

Father Serra and the other padres of the California missions were appalled at the native cultural practices they encountered. In one dance celebrating a young man's ascension to adulthood and its accompanying sexuality, the men sat, circled, playing instruments or singing while the boy danced until he neared collapse. When the boy could dance no longer, a male relative carried the boy on his shoulders and continued the dance. Finally, a female relative of the boy (his sister, his aunt) danced. She lifted her breasts toward the men, and sang. Her lyrics were about male and female genitalia, and the woman sang that she was sexually experienced and ready to do whatever was wanted by any of the men. The Catholic friars, seeing this dance, described it as "an infernal, diabolical invention."

While growing up, the majority of my classmates were Mexican Americans, and it seemed at the time that the Mexicans were cool and us white kids were dorks. To counter my dorkiness I wore shirts buttoned to my neck, a silver crucifix dangling under the stiff pointed collar. My black Z. Cavaricci pants tapered tight to the ankles above my black suede Playboy loafers with the thick and heavy pewter crests stamped to the uppers. I dressed like the Chicano boys around me, who themselves imitated their Pachuco fathers. While hanging out with some of my friends I got into fights and stole packs of Garbage Pail Kids cards from Ken & Sons Produce. I wanted to prove myself, show that I was cool and daring, a badass, even if my friends did not behave in such ways. I stole candy and baseball cards from the Safeway Supermarket in Prunedale when I let Mom slip away to conduct our family's grocery shopping. Even when not at school, when with my little brother and our neighborhood friends, who were all white kids, I wanted to impress them with my daring. All this I did because I assumed that that was what made one cool—like the Mexicans I found myself surrounded by—and not a dumbass. Neither Castroville nor Prunedale—between the two of which my house sat amidst oaks and strawberry fields—had a theater, or a mall, and Mom had to drive us twelve miles into Salinas, or fourteen into Monterey, if we wanted such entertainment. Hence, Mom dropped me, my brother, and our buddy Timmy Boy off at Northridge Mall so we could watch a movie. It was summer in 1989. We watched *Batman*, the one starring Michael Keaton and Jack Nicholson.

After the movie we wandered the mall, scoped out the high school chicks, tooled around Hot Topic, goggle-eyed over the knives and Megadeth T-shirts. We spent our shitty allowances on stickers and the Guns n Roses T-shirt with the band's crossed guns and roses logo, because that was a shirt

Dad would let me wear, unlike the Iron Maiden T's I really wanted, with a ghoulish Eddie screaming and stretching a bony clawed hand out for my soul. It wasn't that my father thought of heavy metal as Satan's music, or anything. He just thought it was tacky and ugly and, looking back, it was, even if that ugly tackiness is badass. Thus, we had with us shopping bags and these bags factor importantly into this narrative.

We ended up at JCPenney, where I talked Timmy Boy and my brother into stealing T-shirts. Genius I was, my plan was simple: walk into dressing room with three T-shirts, put one into Hot Topic shopping bag, walk out of dressing room to replace two T-shirts, leave store, rendezvous outside (except I would've used the verb "meet") in the parking lot.

Imagine Terence Trent D'Arby dropping softly from overhead speakers.

The T-shirt I wanted was of Michael Jordan slam-dunking. I replaced one of Larry Bird and another of Magic Johnson. Who would want their T-shirts? Magic won the MVP that year, but he hadn't any finesse. Not a Jordanesque finesse. Bird was out most the season with heel spurs and he looked almost literally like a bird, with that long face and big nose. No one had style like Jordan, Sir Air, winning his fourth scoring title that year. And Jordan had whooped up on Dominique Wilkins in the Slam Dunk contest two years in a row.

In the dressing room I stashed the Jordan shirt into my bag, then rummaged around. I even removed the shirt I was actually wearing and put it back on, just to make the oomphs and shoves one breathes when one changes clothing.

I waited on a bench outside for my brother and Timmy Boy. It was going late afternoon and the sun hung orange. This skinny mulleted guy in a T-shirt with the sleeves cut off and ripped jeans asked if he could look inside my shopping bag. You ever get that sinking in your gut? It's like the first drop on a roller coaster. I'd gotten myself busted.

Mullet hauled me to a back room where they held shoplifters and called cops. On the way, my arm in his white-knuckled grip, he said, "Don't try to run; I'll tackle your ass down." I was going to turn thirteen years old and was scared shitless. I wasn't running anywhere. Besides, I was chubby and slow. My little league coach wouldn't even let me lead off when I reached base, afraid I would get picked off.

In the back room my brother and Timmy Boy already sat, heads hung, shoulders heaving, which made me go, too. Game over. We were going to juvy. Timmy Boy's stepdad was a cop and his dad was an asshole. No mercy. The tears pooled on the linoleum at my feet. No shirt buttoned to the neck or Playboy loafers could make me look cool.

The head of security wasn't a mullet like the guy who'd caught us; he was a balding man with glasses, and what little hair he did have had grayed some time ago. He had to have been someone's dad, or grandpa, even. He saw what we were: stupid kids—not hoods, not budding criminals—because he asked what we preferred: call the cops, or our parents?

Timmy Boy's dad (his real dad) was furious when he picked us up. He was most mad at me, because I was oldest. He said that I was to set the example. Why wasn't I responsible? What kind of person was I, showing kids how to steal? Turns out my brother had pussed out and didn't go through with it, but security had hauled him off to find us as he wandered around, nine years old and worried where me and Timmy Boy had gone. But Timmy Boy, you might have thought this was the beginning of a lifestyle. His parents divorced and his mom remarried, shacking up with this dude who fathered Timmy Boy's stepbrother and sister, siblings his mother doted on in ways Timmy Boy had only dreamt about. Dick—his father— had also remarried, to a woman with sons a few years older, long-haired hesher kids who smoked weed and spat dirt from the tires of their dirt bikes in Prunedale's hills. One of those guys is now dead: motorcycle accident. I haven't seen Timmy Boy in a long time, but back then, that day, I didn't say anything and sat in the back of the Subaru quietly, worried about what would happen when Mom and Dad saw me.

Home, Mom let me know just how disappointed Jesus was. I cried and cried, and said I was sorry. She handed me my missal, ordered forty Rosaries. She said next Saturday I would go to confession. I hated confession. I can't imagine anyone actually *likes* it.

Mom said, "I don't know what you're going to do when your father gets home."

No amount of Jesus can prepare a child for this dread. I think this is even the subject of a Chris Rock routine, or something like that. My father hardly ever got mad, and he never spanked us. But when he was mad he yelled. But none of those things really scared me. What scared me was some inherent shame—knowing that my mother and father were disappointed in me. The threat that that could happen lay behind my father's yelling, like another person lived inside his voice. That person was one who—even if he did not yell or never touched me—was now disappointed in me. No amount of eternal damnation could compare with this earthly shame.

When my father did come home, he walked into my bedroom. I just let the tears out because there was no way I could stop them. He sat next to me on my bed and said, "You've had a pretty bad day, huh?" I nodded. He said, "Are you sorry for what you did?" I blubbered that I was. Dad said, "You gonna do something stupid like that again?" I shook no, of course, that I would not and I meant it. Dad said, "I guess you've learned your lesson." And he left me alone in my room. I've never stolen anything since.

At Reconciliation the following Saturday I confessed to stealing the T-shirt. I never confessed to my other thefts, of baseball cards or chewing gum, or the butterfly knife I stole out of Chuck Calderon's jean jacket.

In La Plaza de San Francisco in Havana Vieja stands a statue of Blessed Father Fray Junípero Serra and a neophyte boy. The friar's left hand drapes across the boy's shoulder, draws him close. In his right hand, a cross reaches Heavenward. He stares out, slightly upward. The neophyte stares in another direction, his right hand draping along Father Serra's robes, grazing his thigh.

Father Serra was still at Mission San Diego when the Kumeyaay attacked within the first year of its founding. While Serra huddled inside the little chapel, where he offered prayers to God, his servant, Josefa María, a converted Indian from New Spain, ran inside the chapel, blood gushing from his throat. The neophyte fell to his knees in front of Father Serra, spluttering out, "Absolve me, for they have killed me." Blessed Father Fray Junípero Serra administered Josefa Maria's last rites then immediately the boy died. In a later letter to Father Palou, Serra expresses his sadness at not having seen his old friend and companion and how he thinks of the old days when they were able to spend so much time together, and not be separated. He tells Father Palou about the attacks at San Diego, and his sadness at having lost his own Josefa María, the boy he brought from Loreto.

The Kumeyaay, Ipai, Tipai, Chumash, Esselen, Rumsen—all Native Americans of Alta California—shared similarities in their religions. Southern Californian tribes made use of *Datura*, or jimson weed, a hallucinogen, for religious rituals. In the creation, God made brother sky and sister earth. Brother and sister mated, and sister gave birth to all things on Earth, including people, but it was difficult to distinguish people from all other aspects of Earth because everything was alive: granite and obsidian, the Pacific and its waves, the San Diego and Los Angeles Rivers.

Wiyot—a hero—was very powerful, born from lightning, the son of the Creator and a virgin. When Wiyot thought that human women's legs were more beautiful than Frog's, Frog became jealous and poisoned Wiyot. The dying Wiyot went to all the people's villages, and he distributed his power among them. He said, "When I die, I should be cremated." The people built the funeral pyre and the fire. When the fire was ready, and the people about to place Wiyot's body upon it, Coyote came and snatched away Wiyot's heart.

At St. Helena Catholic Church the parish was and still is shepherded by Father Brenkle. Father Brenkle was a huge San Francisco 49ers fan, and in his homily after the Gospel he would sometimes ask God to favor the 49ers that gameday. Grandpa, too, was a huge 49ers fan.

Grandma found religious imagery in natural objects. I think I got that from her, because at my first apartment in Atlanta off my deck stood a tree that seemed to have the image of the crucified Christ in its bark and branches. The main branches branched off, like Jesus's arms on the cross, and at the fork a knot in the tree's bark looked like the bowed head of the dying man, especially at night with the shadows. I told some friends about it who thought I was crazy. We were drinking, of course, if I thought to tell anyone at any time. Once, while at our cabin in Squaw Valley, Granny and I sat on the deck, reading. She lowered her book and stared at the mountains for a while. When I asked what she saw she said, "A tree up on the mountain looks just like Jesus's crown of thorns." I said, "Where?" and looked, but couldn't find it. Granny said, "It's there, if you just keep looking."

I once used this line in a poem: "The trees stood like crosses on the horizon."

When the Kumeyaay attacked, the Spaniards hid their dead to not show the natives that they had succeeded. During the battle, the blacksmith, sporting no armor, roared at the Indians, *God protect us, and slay His enemies!* And he fired his musket into the glop of brown skin. The Spaniards never knew how many Kumeyaay died—for they also carted off their dead—but after a few days, the wounded Indians returned to the mission, seeking help, which the fathers insisted on providing. Blessed Father Fray Junípero Serra said, *Through our charity they will be brought to God.* After months, with so many dead and dying, Portolá gave the order that if the *San Antonio* did not return by the Feast day of Saint Joseph, the presidio and mission would have to be abandoned, and the Sacred Expedition must return over land to Baja California. Father Serra never said anything except in letters to Father Palou, but, had the expedition been abandoned, he would have remained alone among the pagans, to either convert them or die trying. Remarkably, according to the Franciscan history, on the very day, Saint Joseph's day, they spotted sails on the Pacific and hope and relief sparked afresh in each breast, at least for the Spaniards. Who knows what the Kumeyaay thought about any of this.

In *The Godfather* Part III (I know, it's the worst of the trilogy, but still), Michael Corleone sees Cardinal Lamberto, a fictionalized version of the man who will be elected Pope John Paul I. He seeks help from His Eminence in his dealings with Archbishop Gliday, who controls the Vatican Bank. Cardinal Lamberto shows Michael a wet stone and, after he breaks it, says that the water has not penetrated it. He says "The same thing has happened in Europe for centuries. Men have been surrounded by Christianity, but Christ has not penetrated them."

I found my parents' copy of *The Joy of Sex* under their bed. Sketched sexual positions: Missionary, reverse cowgirl, doggy, 69, Spider Monkey. I would take that book into the bathroom in my parents' bedroom and look at the pictures. I don't recall even becoming sexually aroused by the drawings. What was so foreign fascinated me, and I explored it in the bathroom because I'd found this book under my parents' bed (plus all the naked people), so I knew it was meant to be private. One day, Dad knocked on the door, likely because he had to actually *use* his bathroom. A sick nervous feeling shot up through my stomach. I was caught. I tried to hide the book behind the toilet, and came out, after flushing so as to give my bathroom visit the air of actual purpose. Dad looked at me strangely, likely wondering why I was using his bathroom, before he went inside. I tried to walk out of there, but he called me back. This was the one attempt my father made at the "sex talk." He sat me on his bed, *Joy of Sex* in hand. He opened the book and said, "This is what people do when they love each other very much." I looked away. Dad said, "It's okay to look at it." I said, "I don't want to look at it." I was sick to my stomach. I needed to get out of there; I thought I'd throw up. Dad called after me, but I was gone. We never talked about sex again, not until I was an adult.

The mind suffers; the body cries out.

My friend Nick told me how he once ate some jimson weed (*Datura*) and that he hallucinated for three days. His family took a road trip and, while driving over the Sierra Nevada Mountains, he kept seeing dinosaurs roaming the open meadows and charging down the snowy slopes. So it's no wonder that Native Americans who ingested this plant would have used it for religious ceremony.

For the rest of his life Blessed Father Fray Junípero Serra celebrated High Mass on the Feast of St. Joseph, to commemorate the arrival of the *San Antonio* in relief of San Diego.

Prior to Father Serra's naval expedition to Monterey, Father Juan Crespí and Gaspar de Portolá set out overland in search of the port made famous by Juan Sebastián Vizcaíno in 1602. The friar, governor, and soldiers traveled for six months, clambering through the manzanita, scaling the cliffs and mountains of Big Sur, winding through the redwood giants in the valleys, getting lost in the fog. Crespí planted a cross at the mouth of the Carmel River, and another on the Monterey Peninsula, both visible from the sea, but they did not recognize the bay as that which Vizcaíno described and named for the Conde de Monterrey. Serra chalked this up to divine providence, for instead the expedition had discovered what they named the great port of San Francisco de Asís, forty leagues north of where the charts reported Monterey should be found. Portolá, Crespí, and their party returned to San Diego, inscribing on the cross left at Monterey, *The overland expedition from San Diego returned from this place, starving.* Father Serra's disappointment could not be contained, for he said to Portolá, "You come from Rome, but you did not see the Pope." During that conversation, Portolá reeked of the mules he and his men had barbecued daily for food while retracing 480 miles to San Diego.

Father Serra covered the above distance by sea aboard the *San Antonio* in a one-month voyage. He and the soldiers ate beans, rice, a little chocolate. When Father Serra arrived at the place where the charts indicated Monterey should have been, where Father Crespí had planted his cross and celebrated mass, the Blessed Father found the cross still standing, littered on and about it by arrows thrust into the ground and feathers. A necklace of still-fresh sardines hung from a nearby branch, and mussels piled at the cross base—offerings from natives, for they witnessed the veneration that the father and soldiers bestowed on the symbol and recognized it as a talisman for a god. Later, after the Indians learned enough Spanish at the missions, they told the fathers that at night the cross glowed and seemed to grow in size and ascend into the sky. The Indians wanted to make peace offerings to the cross. This is the word of the fathers.

Sebastián Vizcaíno detailed a port sheltered from all winds. Who knows what Portolá and Crespí expected, for Monterey Bay is large: 350 square statute miles. But it is not as sheltered as San Francisco and San Pablo bays. The Marin Headlands and the San Francisco peninsula make for a narrow one mile channel as access to the Pacific, whereas the mouth of Monterey Bay yawns a good twenty-five miles across, and Monterey Canyon, dropping to over two miles below the surface, generates strong currents. Nevertheless, Father Serra recognized the bay as that which Vizcaíno discovered, and there, beneath a towering oak the Father and soldiers celebrated mass.

Bears are, generally, afraid of fire. Once, at my family's cabin in Squaw Valley, California, in the Sierra Nevada Mountains, I saw a bear. I had bought Subway for dinner, and after finishing it I threw my wrapper into the garbage can on the deck. There wasn't any food leftover in that wrapper or bag, but that does nothing for the smell of Eat Fresh, and by that I mean freshly baked dough and fresh ingredients, made in front of the customer to my exact specifications, by Subway Sandwich Artists. I was watching Discovery Channel. There is no small irony in how I was *Discovering my world*, or *The thrill of my Discovery*, and I was thinking *Let's all discover*... And then: *what the fuck was that?* A large crash sounded from the deck. Dogs freely roam the valley, so I assumed a pack had tumbled the garbage. I ventured outside to right the can, the lid of which remained intact. As soon as I returned in front of the tube the crash sounded again. This time garbage spread across the driveway. I said, *Goddamnit*, and started cleaning it up when I heard grunting. To my left a rather large black bear had its nose stuck in a tuna can. He couldn't have been more than ten feet away. Back inside I grabbed the barbecue's lighter fluid and a log from the fireplace, doused and lit said log and tossed it into the driveway. The bear ran away. I sometimes wished that I had lighter fluid with me while there in Georgia so that I might toss burning logs at potential attacking bears as I romped wildly through the forest, burning down the mountains.

Our Lady of Refuge Catholic Church held an annual fundraiser, The Ham Dinner. They still do. But, I like to think of it as The Big Bear Dinner. And in this fiction, I think that maybe they called it that because of the story of the

Valle de Los Osos and the missions, and that would mean someone knew a good deal about early California history. In both the real and fictional versions, the proceeds from your ticket went to the church. All of this is real: Dinner was a slab of ham, along with mostachioli and marinara, salad, and candied yams. No bear was served, either a plate or on one. What's weirder is that the young lady chosen to be that year's Artichoke Festival Queen appeared at the dinner, and she donned a crude mask, made to look like Miss Piggy from the Muppets. At The Big Bear Dinner it would be a Fozzy Bear mask. Either way, a raffle was held. The Queen assisted in this task: kissing winners, Fozzie Bear mask, Miss Piggy mask, hip-hugging dress, manicured nails.

L. Trousset's 1870 painting, *Father Serra's Landing Place, or Celebration of the First Mass*, depicts a coast oak at Monterey. The Spanish flag drapes at the painting's center, held aloft by a kneeling soldier. Also raised are Blessed Father Fray Junípero Serra's arms, Eucharist to the sun, like the Father's eyes, as he sings, "Take this bread and eat it, for this is my body." Fathers Juan Crespí and Buenaventura Sitjar kneel at opposite sides of the altar, sheltered by the ship's sail that dangles from the oak's branches. The leatherjackets square the scene, gun barrels resting like palisades. In the distant bay the *San Antonio* floats, backgrounded by the sand dunes of what would later become the city of Seaside, and the rolling golden foothills of Mount Toro. And from that barge a cannon will fire in response to the ringing bell, and to the muskets' repeat. And what must the Indian, a Rumsen, be thinking, at the painting's lower left corner, as he peers into the scene from the seclusion of a boulder? What fears or hopes, or curiosity must gird him?

Does he know what lay in wait, the syphilis and measles, the death of his culture?

The sentence, *Take this and drink from it, for this is my blood*, makes me think of a tick, and I am thinking of ticks due to the fact that I write this while in the Appalachian Mountains, where there are ticks.

My parents made me take a test, so I took it[8]. I did not know what the test was for. Then the school accepted me. For the fourth grade I attended Sacred Heart Catholic School in Salinas. Mrs. Martineau, my third grade teacher at Castroville Elementary, was very excited when I told her that I would attend this new school. I don't remember why I would've told her about any of this, although I do know that I loved her as a teacher. She was grandmotherly, with glasses and coifed silver hair. She gave me a copy of C.S. Lewis's *The Lion, the Witch, and the Wardrobe*, perhaps my introduction to literature, if you didn't count Dr. Seuss. Maybe Mrs. Martineau was herself a Catholic, and that was why she gave me C.S. Lewis books? I hated fourth grade at Sacred Heart. I left the friends with whom I had attended school since kindergarten in Castroville, and became the outcast new kid in Salinas. Alone, I'd lean against a pole during recess and lunch. I faked stomachaches so Mom would pick me up and take me with her to the travel agency

---

8   "Sacred Heart School uses an achievement test of basic skills and a school-prepared test as part of the admittance process. Applicants are accepted only after all entrance requirements have been met. Registration preference is given to siblings of currently enrolled students, members of Sacred Heart Parish, siblings of currently enrolled students who are members of neighboring Catholic parishes, Catholic applicants from neighboring parishes, and applicants of other faith traditions." http://www.shschool.com/

where she worked down the street, or sometimes she drove me thirteen miles back home. Sometimes I was not faking my sickness. Fourth grade was the year I discovered my colesteatoma. I didn't know it was colesteatoma. All I knew was that I went deaf in my left ear, and I sometimes got dizzy. Also, at Sacred Heart we went to church every day. Seriously, we attended all five days of the week and, of course, I went on Sunday with my family, too. This did nothing for my piety. In fact my faith floundered under such indoctrination. The church and school compound was arranged not unlike a mission: the church took up the city block's corner, with the school's administrative buildings and classrooms walling in a courtyard that contained the recess and physical education playing fields. We had music class where we learned to sing for God in the choir. Eventually I made a few friends. One invited me to his birthday party. His name was Jaime, a Mexican boy, and so his name was pronounced High-May. I returned to Castroville for the fifth grade, and I never saw Jaime again.

What I miss about California: cliffs, and golden rolling hills, blue sea, kelp. None of that here in the north Georgia mountains. In Georgia, they say, Drive Safe, because mountain people don't know how to drive. And this makes me laugh because the Appalachians are old mountains, like 100 million year-old mountains. The road out of my little valley and the highway into Dillard from Mountain City and Clayton was four lanes and nearly flat. But try driving Highway 1 in Big Sur after two hours at the Boar's Head Saloon. The narrow road twists along cliffs that drop hundreds of feet to the rocky coast where the the waves crash and splash. Now *that's* driving.

Since I'm being honest: in the eleven days since I'd begun my cabin stay in order to write, and endured my panic attack, I had so far consumed 115 beers, a fifth of Makers Mark, a fifth of Kettle One, half a bottle of Martini and Rossi Dry Vermouth, a fifth of Cazadores Tequila, and five bottles of wine. I agree with the physicians that such behavior is not healthy.

In the fourth Station of the Cross, you meet your mother, who remains perpetually blue robed, cowl-sheathed, as she comforts you in this hour of your death. You appear resolute, motioning your mother off, to say, *Nothing more can you do for me.* You push away your mother for that is what all children must do with all mothers. Your shoulders hold up pure white robes, despite having been beaten, stripped, flogged, held as prisoner. Your shoulders and face sit white as alabaster, scratchless. Not a drip of dried blood or caked dirt mars you. In Matisse's study, the figures of you and your mother remain faceless, crossless, a tender meeting of featureless bodies.

Saint Charles, or San Carlos de Borromeo, a Medici: namesake of Monterey, California's presidio and mission, founded by Father Serra in 1770. San Carlos's uncle: Pope Pius IV. Carlos worked through a strain of plague in Milan in the late 16th century, blessing the sick, dying, and dead. He helped found the Golden League in Switzerland, an Inquisition-like institution that worked against the Reformation, and burned heretics at the stake. San Carlos de Borromeo is known for his humility and wisdom, and is venerated even in England, a country that, during Carlos's own lifetime, actively became anti-Catholic. San Carlos was of rich, noble, and influential birth. Pius IV forced him to live lavishly, to demonstrate the Church's power. Did Carlos complain? Father Serra, himself once Inquisitor in Nueva España, lived to emulate this man of the cloth.

Blue robed, Sor María de Jésus de Ágreda appeared to the Jumanos of the Texas panhandle and of Oklahoma. She said, "Go to the pueblo mission and be not afraid. The fathers will come to your people." Meantime the body of the venerable mother María remained ensconced in her Ágredan Abby. The missionary fathers hiked the heathen plains. When Jumanos approached, naked, bearing rude lashed crosses, the fathers baptized over 10,000 natives. The two fathers, left in the roughhewn chapel fashioned from oak and willow of the open plains, died alone of loneliness, starvation, poisoning, bison stampede, murder by natives: all of the above.

My father and I, along with other members of the Chumash Tribe of the Salinas YMCA Indian Guides, camped at Lake San Antonio summers. Live oaks and deer skeletons covered the rolling hills. Fur still clung to rotting shoulders, a teeth-bared and sun-bleached grin. A rattler slithered into camp and we circled it, watching, before it flashed past, under our tent. I didn't want to sleep in there that night, but Dad said the snake would be gone. Fishing, Dad tossed his line into the lake and whipped out a golden flipping thing: a bluegill. Stinking in the cooler, and stinking up the van, we tossed it. This was all on traditional Salinan Indian land where there never would've been a lake at all before the Americans constructed the dam out of earth. We white people—meaning me, Dad, the other sons and fathers with us—called ourselves "Chumash" for fun, though in real life the Chumash were a highly developed culture that spanned the mid and southern California coast.

After celebrating High Mass in the foundation ceremony of Mission San Carlos de Borromeo de Monterey, Father Serra explored the surrounding countryside. He found over the hill of the peninsula the river that Sebastián Viscaíno's Carmelite friars had named for their order, El Río Carmelo, and where it trickles into the Pacific. There on the flat and fertile flood plain spread with chaparral, the *padre presidente* planned to eventually move his mission. Pines and oaks fell for the chapel. Junípero Serra explored Carmel Valley, through which the river twists up into the Santa Lucia Mountains. He traveled south to the Valley de Los Robles, where he discovered another river flowing north, strong in July. Father Serra named this inland river the San Antonio.

What a difference between San Diego and Monterey, the former choked by chaparral of manzanita and yucca, the Torrey pines gathered in wind-gusted groves, constant sun beating its golden club upon the priests' tonsured heads. Then they came to Monterey, swaddled in fog, the cypress and pines dripping, clinging to the cold dew-kissed rocks, cliffs tumbling to a roiling sea. How could Father Serra have even thought of the two places as inhabiting the same country, a country he called California?

For those who have not already noticed adobe and abode are anagrams.

The early missions were not made of adobe, but of earth and wood and thatch.

In San Diego the thatched roofs were of *Setaria parviflora*, marsh bristlegrass. Among other plants endemic to Presidio Hill and Old Town in San Diego: *Conium maculatum* (poison hemlock), *Amblyopappus pusillus* (dwarf coastweed), *Artemesia douglasiana* (dream plant), *Artemesia palmeri* (San Diego sagebrush), *Bidens pilosa* (Spanish needle), *Centaurea melitensis* (tocalote), *Isocoma menziesii var. menziesii* (white-flowered goldenbush), *Lasthenia glabrata ssp. coulteri* (goldfields), *Anredara cordifolia* (Madeira vine), *Lotus heermanii var. heermanii* (wooly lotus), *Geranium anemonifolium* (Canary Island geranium), and *Phacelia stellaris* (star phacelia).

In the beginning the earth was empty and formless, except for the chaparral, the sand dunes, and the bay of San Diego. There were no fresh fruits or vegetables, and so men suffered from scurvy. Their shrunken and bleeding gums, the orifices of their eyes, noses, and assholes became entryways for infection. The world hung with the odor of decay, of both human body and human waste. Junípero Serra's hands—all the Spaniards' hands—caked with dirt so that it drew lines in the palm lines. The dirt worked its way under fingernails. While back in Mexico, in the Sierra Gorda, Father Serra folded cloth upon his shoulder to level his short height as he hefted beams to assist in the erection of the colossal stone church at Jalpan de Sierra, and now years later, in San Diego, Monterey, and San Antonio his work ethic had not aged with his body. The felled trees he huffed to heave away, though subcutaneous splinters sprouted septicemia. But he would not fall ill, and lived to 1784, fifteen years after he arrived in San Diego.

In Padua in Italy in a reliquary sits Saint Anthony's tongue. Said tongue is incorruptible, as in it has not decayed in the intervening 784 years since Anthony's death. Father Serra revered Anthony for his oratorical powers. Under Pope Gregory IX, Antonio di Padua composed saints' feast day sermons for which he gained fame. Father Serra himself was famous for dropping his habit to his waist, baring his chest, striking it with a heavy stone, all while reciting the Act of Contrition. San Antonio's—for which the mission in California and the city in Texas are both named—tongue is blackened and glistening. Upon exhumation, it was seen that Father Serra's remains remained quite corruptible.

Along the banks of the San Antonio River, Father Serra, along with Fathers Buenaventura Sitjar and Miguel Pieras, consecrated the ground and erected the foundation cross in founding Mission San Antonio de Padua, third of the missions of Nueva California. In celebration, before the High Mass, Father Serra had the main bell strung upon the branch of a live oak and, ringing it, he hollered to the empty flat of the valley studded with yet more live oaks: "Come! Come you pagans and receive the faith of Jesus Christ!" When his fellow friars asked their prelate why he exerted himself so, in a land devoid of other humans, he replied, "Just as Sor María de Jésus de Ágreda, that venerable mother, brought the Holy faith to the gentiles of Nuevo México, here also this bell cries, beckoning to the heathen of this sierra." After the gospel, when Father Serra turned from the oaken altar to deliver his homily, he spied a solitary Salinan Indian in view of the rite. The Blessed Father exclaimed, "I foresee that this Mission San Antonio will reap a great harvest for the Lord, for the fruits of paganism are already at hand!" And he gave to the native gifts of beads to entice him to return to the mission and to bring his friends.

Speaking of fruit, Father Francisco Palou details the abundant foods available to the Salinan Indians of el Valle de los Robles, where the fathers situated Mission San Antonio de Padua. For the natives' sustenance the Earth provided rabbits, squirrels, chipmunks, deer, geese, ducks, snakes, lizards, clams and mussels, trout, piñon pine, and acorns. Palou described the great oak-filled plains as if they resembled the landscaped parks of Europe, for the grass grew low beneath the trees. The natives systematically burned the grass to facilitate the acorn harvest, but the Europeans did not see this and assessed the tribes as cultureless heathen.

At Lake San Antonio, Dad said that the Indians ate acorns. So, I tried some, after gathering and shelling them. Dad laughed when I grimaced at the bitter taste, and the way the nut dried my mouth. I said, "How could they eat that." Dad said, "When you're an Indian you eat what you have to." Much later I learned how Native Americans prepared acorns, so making them palatable.

Not long after I wrote this, my dad suffered a stroke, and the food he chewed as he recovered in his hospital bed, shoved to his mouth's left side—the side affected by his damaged brain—stayed there, his cheeks puffed like a chipmunk's, until we instructed my dad to tongue it out.

Acorns are high in tannic acid, as are walnuts or pecans, and that's what leaves the dry film rimming the inside of your mouth. Native Californians learned to leach their acorns of the tannins, after having harvested in the fall, when the seeds have ripened and fallen from the trees. Ripe acorns typically fall cap-intact. Capless acorns are usually wormy, the wiggles of a worm wrenching the acorn from its cap prematurely. Ripened acorns are golden and shiny, their shells uncracked and whole. After harvest, the acorns were dried, shelled, and ground. Salinan mizzen sites speckle arroyos in the Santa Lucia foothills. Large flat boulders pocked from these ancient Californians' labors tell stories from before the coming of the Spanish Empire. The acorns were ground to a grit-like consistency, or a very fine powder for baking into loaves. The acorn meal was then taken to the sand at the nearby arroyo. Natives heaped the sand into mounds and dug out cavities, filling said cavities with acorn meal. The clear cold spring water washed out the tannins into the sand below, a natural sieve. To cook, Salinans used water-tight cooking baskets which they filled with the prepared acorn meal and water. They heated select clean round rocks in a fire to very high temperatures, which they stirred into the water and meal in their cooking baskets, removing cooled rocks and returning them to the fire for heating in rotation. Quickly, the water came to a boil. The natives cooked their meal in a variety of thin, soup-like, or oatmeal-like consistencies. They added salt and elderberries to the mixture for flavor.

Despite the abundance of said nature's fruits, the Spanish missions of Nuevo California, because of the Europeans' insistence on "civilized" agriculture, were in the midst of a severe famine within the first year of existence.

On the DVD Menu for *The Godfather* the climactic chapter is titled "Baptism and Murder."

A Salvation Army homeless shelter in Spokane, Washington turned away a family of Chippewa Indians, refusing to accept their tribal IDs as valid. The poor family scrounged and borrowed enough cash for a Motel 6, but there still wasn't enough room. While the mother, father, and two kids slept in the hotel, the grandparents stayed in the car. That winter night in Spokane the temperature dropped to -5° F.

If I thought hard enough about it, I was able to turn the terrors into lucid dreams. The terrors were terrible: footsteps approaching my turned back, while I lay on the bed, and I felt the hand belonging to whomever owned those feet on my back. I knew that this was a dream, even if it felt so real. So I thought about how I wanted to play with my cat, my cat who—even in this dream—I knew had been dead for over a year. And he bounced around a corner of the cabin into the bedroom, prancing toward me, like he would when he was happy I'd come home from work. He rolled onto his back so I could scratch his belly. I cried, and when I came to consciousness the pillow was soaked with my tears.

Lake San Antonio looked like a place where Indians could still live: oaks and deer, no rows of tract housing in sight, not even a Safeway supermarket within thirty miles. As a member of the Chumash Tribe of the Salinas YMCA Indian Guides, I liked to imagine the Salinans still romped the hills, though I didn't know then to call them Salinans. They were headbanded and leather vested, just like us boys. Though our headbands Velcroed together, and our vests were stitched from corduroy. To round out the stereotype, the feathers shoved into our headbands were dyed bright red and gold. This was how we honored a decimated culture, a nearly extinct people. The YMCA Indian Guides' website explains the organization's symbols, blazoned on said headband that wrapped my head. The central circle symbolized the "Great Spirit," a necessarily monotheistic interpretation of native spirituality—thus safe for American children.

When I returned home from the mountains, back to my wife in Atlanta, baseball season had ended, and the leaves had fully changed, painting the city red and yellow. But before that the Braves were in the running for the postseason, heading up against the Philadelphia Phillies for first place in the NL East. When the Braves get a base hit, a homerun, sometimes even a walk, a comical 1950s cowboy and Indian Hollywood Western theme sprouts from the stadium speakers. Above the left-centerfield bleachers, at an oversized drum, an employee sporting a headdress and drumsticks pounds a rhythm, while the crowd's palms like tomahawks chop the air in the Tomahawk Chop. Meantime everyone chants a chant one only hears in said Hollywood films.

The San Diego Padres.

When natives came to be baptized at the missions they also immediately became charges of the padres. The Franciscans forced their Indians to learn Spanish and the Catholic Doctrina. Each mission's Indian population erected the mission buildings, was taught the labors of agriculture, and thus the native lost knowledge of his traditional ways of life.

Howka, M'am maj? Xmath mixi? M'ay mey miá? Hola, ¿donde va Ud.? ¿Cual es el nombre Ud.? ¿Donde vives? En la ranchería, el reduccion. Inyage NaWere, Anam Asoo. Tengo hambre. ¿Teines algo de comer? No hay nada de comer. Los misionarios no tienen nada de comer.

In this famine, when mission food stores at San Diego dwindled to their cows' milk, starving soldiers scoured the hills, their horses gaunt, the hills emaciated.

In 1771 Father Serra ordered Fathers Angel Somera and Pedro Cambon north from Mission San Diego along the trail, so that they might found Mission San Gabriel Arcángel at the banks of El Rio de Los Temblores, on a plain that sloped from the mountains to the sea. The padres and their *escalta* trudged through the chaparral, wary of the rattle of rattlesnakes, dozing dark nights swimming with coyote whoops. When the native Tongvas approached, screeching, brandishing their war clubs, bows and arrows, Father Somera withdrew from a pack upon his mule the oil of *Nuestra Señora de Los Dolores*, brandishing it in the pre-LA sunlight. The Indians threw down their weapons, and ran forward to the friar. They fell to their knees, spilled open leather pouches, their offerings of pine nuts and dried fish as sacrifices to the god before them.

Museums and churches in Russia are the same: wafts of wax and old books. In the Russian Museum, St. Petersburg: a 12th century wood panel depicting the Archangel Gabriel. In the churches, or museums (sometimes both together) the faithful spied me, chins tilting sidelong, when I genuflected. Excusing myself to my wife—we're not religious—I said, "respect." The wife only said, "It's okay. You were confirmed, right?"

Xielolixii—Iron Woman—her family is the Bear Clan of the Salinan Indians. She lies in Monterey County, where before it was any county, her ancestors had lived. Now, beyond her 70th year, bear claws tattoo down her chin.

In Claudio Boltiansky's "Virgin and Child," Mary prays over her sleeping Messiah. Palms pressed, fingers splayed—*here is the steeple, here is the church*—her blue robes spill, a Pacific cascading the crags of her shoulders. Eyes downcast, mouth set in meditation, her skin glows pale. The child, covered in white linen, radiates: a sun, golden glowing locks, a hint of halo.

These natives—Kumeyaay, Tongva, Esselen, Rumsen, Salinan—having never seen a Western style oil, beheld a window unto the world from which gods looked out and back. At the pine palisades that walled the mission, women gathered for a glimpse. The fathers brought forth the painting to the stockade, where the women thrust their breasts through the narrows of the fence posts, attempting to suckle the pale child upon his holy mother's lap.

Walking Castroville's streets after school I got into fights but mostly watched other boys scrabbling on the asphalt. I went to Burger King for Whoppers. My friends and I cussed regularly, unless we were on the same block on which sat the church. My friend Antonio once admonished me when I said, "damn," while strutting the sidewalk alongside the church. He said, "Jaime"—pronounced Hi-May, which was what all the Mexicans called me—"you're crazy, eh. Don't cuss at the church." I said, "We're not *in* church." And I could not have known that his use of the preposition "at" meant "here," or "near." Once we'd crossed the street, Tony crossed himself and said, "Damn dude, you're fuckin crazy!"

Father Serra was astonished to learn of the Sacred Expedition's soldiers committing grave mortal sins. Said soldiers had marched north from Mexico through the arid Baja peninsula to San Diego. Then again, some more had gone farther north to El Rio Hondo and to Mission San Gabriel Arcángel. All these thousands of miles these men passed through womanless. One soldier—we'll call him Juan María—raped a Tongva chief's wife. The chief and men from his village and other nearby villages armed themselves for vengeance. Juan María and another soldier put the horses out to pasture and then the Tongva attacked. The chief took a musket ball to the head and died instantly, the men whom he'd called for help scattering. The Spaniards beheaded the dead chief and paraded the trophy around the mission, displaying it upon the spiked end of a stockade piling. The rapist Juan María was never punished for his crime, but was instead removed to Monterey, where he could be maintained under the medieval eyes of Blessed Father Fray Junípero Serra. Over time, the Tongva forgot about their chief's murder, and even his own son came to be baptized at Mission San Gabriel Arcángel.

Upon reaching the harbor of San Diego, Father Serra scouted the level fertile swath not far from El Rio de San Diego, and there he ordered the soldiers to fell the trees to be fashioned into the foundation cross. He then consecrated ground, cross, and mission: San Diego de Alcalá. Upon an oaken altar Father Serra placed an oil of *nuestra señora, la madre de dios*. A woman clothed with the sun, the moon beneath her feet, twelve stars crowning her head, her belly distended with child. A seven-headed dragon attacks the venerable mother, but the Archangel Michael, sword ready, protects her. Father Serra and his painting showed the *soldados de cuera* the prelate's mission: defeat the beast of the apocalypse, and spread the good Word of God.

In 1960 Sister Mary Boniface Dyrda prayed for the intercession of Blessed Father Fray Junípero Serra while on her deathbed at DePaul Hospital in St. Louis. The nun had been diagnosed with lupus after her body one day went numb. Doctors thus removed her spleen and the Franciscan Sister's weight dropped to eighty-six pounds. She prayed to the Apostle of California, believing it the *presidente's* time to demonstrate his place next to God in Heaven. A couple weeks later Sister Mary returned to her convent, cured. Hers would be the first of the required two miracles for the Blessed Father's canonization. Pope John Paul II beatified Father Serra on September 17, 1987. From the brome-covered hillside where the native Rumsen might have once roamed, before the syphilis and measles that killed most of them—brought by Father Serra, and his fellow Spaniards—I watched the Pope and this mass then fell asleep next to my mother.

In the fifth Station of the Cross: behold Simon of Cyrene forced to help Jesus with his burden. The Second Treatise of the Great Seth, a Gnostic text, says that Jesus—because he was never of flesh, only took on the appearance of the flesh—was not the man crucified, that it had to have been Simon of Cyrene who did the dying.

Father Serra's first baptism in Alta California went horribly awry (non-Spanish speakers, unfamiliarity with Catholic Rite). Eventually, though, natives came to the missions for baptism of their own accord. No going home. *Soldados de cuera* hunted escaped neophytes and brought them back, ropes around their necks, and at musket-point, or by way of pinched ears. Returned "escapees" were publicly flogged and spent a day in the stocks.

Among Blessed Father Fray Junípero Serra's medieval forebears was John Duns Scotus, whose theological musings on the miraculous truth of the Virgin Mary's Immaculate Conception the *presidente* held close to his own battered heart.

That theological point of view, having been problematic for some centuries, even up to the time of Father Serra, was that Mary the Mother of Jesus was herself conceived by God to be free of original sin, even if Mary had been born of parents who were themselves born with original sin, who had sexual intercourse to become pregnant in the way that nature commands. The philosophical problem with this theology lies in the saving death of Jesus. Why would Jesus' death be necessary if already there existed a pure being, conceived by God, in the form of Mary? Duns Scotus claimed that Mary only gained salvation through Jesus' death, and that with her foreknowledge of future events—revealed to her by the Archangel Gabriel—her salvation came *in anticipation* of the crucifixion. One learns all the necessary theology concerning this dogma by enrolling in courses in Mariology at Saint Allesio Falcioneri, the Marianum Pontifical School, in Rome.

Because of Duns Scotus's later reputation—that his philosophical points could not stand the onslaught of the Enlightenment—those who adhered to his dictates were called Duns, from which "dunce" derives, meaning "a dull-witted, ignorant, or stupid person."

Gerard Manley Hopkins wrote a sonnet, "Duns Scotus's Oxford," but it has little to do with me, or with Blessed Father Fray Junípero Serra, being primarily a poem about Oxford University in England. However, Hopkins's poem is not wholly dismissible as an irregular Petrarchan Sonnet. In the first stanza the line syllable lengths run 1: eleven; 2: seventeen; 3: fifteen; and 4: twelve. The second stanza follows a more or less traditional ten-syllable line length. Then, in the third and fourth stanzas Hopkins lets loose yet again, "unraveling" his syllables at will. The poem in fact reads like a pre-perfected form of Hopkins's famous "sprung verse" from which a poem like "God's Grandeur" is exemplary. Hopkins makes light of his "unraveller['s] . . . not / Rivaled insight," according to the folks in Rome and Athens, heads of the Catholic Church and Eastern Orthodox Church, respectably, those who condemned Duns's thinking when it came to the most holy virgin we know. And of the closing line—"Who fired France for Mary without spot"—we can say that Hopkins certainly prescribed to the Dunsian perspective on the Immaculate Conception.

At the Lullian University in Palma, Blessed Father Fray Junípero Serra occupied the Duns Scotus chair in philosophy.

I think my mother had the concept (sigh) of the Immaculate Conception all wrong. I always thought it had to do with

Mary conceiving Jesus miraculously as a virgin. Pope Pius IX decreed that, "in the first moment of [Mary's] conception . . . [she] was preserved exempt from all stain of original sin."[9] However, in light of the etymology of "concept," stemming from the Middle Latin *conceptum*, from the present participle of *concipere*, to take in, which translated to the Old French *conceveir*, I can conceive that my mother's conception of that one Immaculate Conception was not altogether incorrect.

I wonder does this translate to the Immaculate *Reception*, where it's unclear if Terry Bradshaw's pass first hit Frenchy Fuqua of the Steelers, or Jack Tatum of the Raiders, or if it hit both of them. Prior to 1978, if a pass was touched first by an offensive player—and touched only by that player— said player then became the only eligible receiver *to take in* that pass. So, are the Steelers free of the sin of scoring a touchdown unfairly?

The soldiers in George Orwell's essay "A Hanging" hope to quickly dispatch of their prisoner. The dog that jauntily bounces up to them, distracting them from their duty, angers the guards. This dog, tongue lapping, tail wagging, accompanies the party to the man's praying death, whereat even the dog seems aware of the seriousness of the act, his gamboling and gleeful yipping ceased. After the condemned man's lifeless legs swing, his executioners drink whiskey and tell nervous jokes.

My first communion missal condensed the gospels' Passion to a single narrative. This singularity made for a good story: both a sad and happy ending. Jesus, betrayed by Judas, goes

9   from The Catholic Encyclopedia: http://www.newadvent.org/cathen/07674d.htm

to his death. The Romans scourge his back with scourges. The march to Golgotha, with the wiping of Jesus' face, Simon of Cyrene's help, meeting Mary Magdalene and Mary, the mother of Jesus. Nails driven through hands and feet. Blood trailing down the cross's splintered length. Jesus dies and is buried. On the third day, Mary the Mother of Jesus and Mary Magdalene encounter a risen man. In body, Jesus remains forty days—so happy to have him returned! Yet so sad, for his family and his apostles who lose their friend, and get him back, only to lose him again. But like all good stories, he remains in spirit, and the Holy Spirit does, in fact, descend upon these, his lofty disciples.

One can read the same basic plot in Roger Spottiswoode's *Turner and Hooch*. Police officer Scott Turner (Tom Hanks) is transformed (or converted) by a big, messy, rambunctious Dogue de Bordeaux, who helps him solve a murder. Sacrificing himself, Hooch takes a bullet at the climax and as a result later dies. But he has already impregnated another dog (conveniently provided by the town veterinarian, who likewise conveniently plays Turner's love interest). Dénouement: little Hooches carry on their father's legacy of annoying Officer Turner. In other words, Hooch lives on through his offspring. Resurrection!

Turner and Hooch was shot in Pacific Grove, California, on the Monterey Peninsula, about six miles from Mission San Carlos de Borromeo del Rio Carmelo, and about three miles from the Royal Presidio Chapel.

Serra scholar Father Zephyrn Engelhardt wrote that, like Officer Turner, Father Serra was not fond of dogs.

Actually, that last part's not true, but what is true is that in the beginning of the 20th century, Franciscan Father Zephyrin Engelhardt, known as the authority on California mission history, wrote to John Steven McGroarty for godspeed in his writing of *The Mission Play*, a sentimental epic starring Father Serra as a fiery padre desperate to defend his neophyte maidens' honor against rapist secular Spanish authorities. Father Engelhardt was especially pleased that McGroarty represented the Blessed Father without "everlasting, silly femininity."

One-time editor of the *LA Times*, Charles Fletcher Lummis described McGroarty's play, its treatment of Native Californians, and its historical inaccuracies thus: "Father Serra didn't teach the California Indians to weave dam [sic] bad Navajo blankets!"

The Mission Play: three acts: the Sacred Expedition's near failure, with its sailors and soldiers dying of starvation and scurvy; the missions' rise to greatness; and the missions' fall to ruin in the hands of the newly independent Mexican government. *The Mission Play* was performed at Mission San Gabriel 3,268 times to over 200,000 spectators.

In San Diego, Monterey, and San Gabriel—as well as in all the as-of-yet unfounded missions—mass was sung daily and neophyte attendance mandatory. The fathers called roll each morning and each native came forward after hearing his or her name to kiss the padre's hand. Absent Indians found on mission grounds were driven to mass by way of a long stick that the friars also used to smack neophytes about the ears should they be caught nodding off during the service.

Sunday mornings Mom or Dad woke me and my brother and sister using the same tactic deployed on school days: blinds flung open to sunlight, windows opened for cold air, comforters snatched from shivering bodies. My mom was late for *everything*. Even as an adult, once, when home visiting, I drove her to work and she was late and yelling at me, for whenever she's late it's someone else's fault. If I need her to be on time for anything I lie about said time, giving her an hour's leeway. So far, that's been successful. As a kid, Mom got particularly angry when late for church. She'd say that we wouldn't be late if she "didn't have to clean up after you kids!" We wore our clichéd "Sunday best" to church. I asked why. Mom said, "Don't you think God cares how you dress in His house?" Around the eighth grade I got wise, arguing that God would not care what I wore, as it says so right there in the Bible: "You cannot serve God and wealth." So why should I dress in my best, but instead be meek and humble in front of God. Mom, still wiser, said that if I wanted to look like a bum in front of my friends and my priest, then that was up to me. So compliance with community pressure is always stronger than the ephemeral. I'd like to think Mom thought God would be angry when we arrived at church late. More likely, Mom did not like the faces turned back at the creak of the doors as they opened to the nave's inner sanctum upon our entry while Father Scott monotoned the last of the Kyrie.

Writing to Father Fray Francisco Palou, Father Junípero Serra says, "The occasion might arise in which we might personally embrace each other in the middle or toward the end of September." No doubt this longing is a result of pure loneliness, living on the New Spanish frontier, surrounded by what the fathers perceived as barbaric strangers jibbering a language wholly foreign and godless. But this tenderness underlying Serra's letter goes beyond wishing for the familiar: a desire to touch flesh to flesh, soft whiskered cheeks brushing together like Santa Ana winds, coarse Franciscan robes against fingertips, soft Spanish lips.

In Saint Helena there was no video rental store. We plucked movies from the shelves of the public library where the selection was exactly the kind of selection you get at all public libraries. If the videos actually worked—and without adjusting the tracking—it was a good day. We made it through about three minutes of *Ferris Bueller's Day Off*, to where Matthew Broderick's lathering in the shower and says, "I do have a test today; that wasn't bullshit." Grandpa ripped the cassette from the machine. We stomped our feet. Grandpa said, "You're not watching this garbage on Easter Sunday." I was twelve, which made my sister nine and bespectacled, and my brother eight, a towhead. Mom laughed when we protested, and she said, "It's Grandpa's house, and that's the rule." I would be sixteen when I finally got past Ferris's soaped noggin and on to other antics.

Blessed Father Fray Junípero Serra raised the Eucharistic goblet to his lips, and candlelight danced on the blood's tiny waves. Incense clouded the church so completely that some of the Pame natives grew nauseated. So, too, felt Blessed Father Fray Junípero Serra later that night, as he bent over a ceramic bowl and vomited blood, not only the Lord's, but his own, for poison had laced the sacred vessel into which he poured the sacrament. The physician tending to the sick prelate urged him to take the remedy he'd prepared. But Father Serra refused, said that he would pray, for he had never taken any medicine in his life, and he never would.

Fathers Juan Crespí and Francisco Gomez had hiked from San Diego in the south, crashing through brambles, till they came upon the dying Indian children. The mother tried to get the one, a little brown baby, to suckle from her breast, the child's tiny ribs striping the thin skin of her abdomen. The Fathers filled an abalone shell with Holy water then blessed and baptized the two María Magdalena and Margarita, the first natives baptized in Alta California. Then the baby died.

Saddling their horses and hoofing into the wild countryside, out of priests' sight and earshot, *soldados de cuera* lassoed Native women and dragged them down, dusting shins and thighs, bloodying knees. Rough hands stroked back sea otter capes. Hissed *español* and whiskered cheeks rubbed skin raw, hard cocks pressed against native vaginas and anuses. Left shuddering under the manzanita, the sight of a horse's backside, the Texcuco and Spanish shoulders black in the sun, the only sound: that of the rapist clopping away, back to the mission where the priests prayed Hail Mary Full of Grace.

In artistic renditions of the Annunciation, Mary, flush in lavish blue robes, sits or kneels in a room vaulted and draped. Said room's furniture is intricately carved. The Virgin has situated herself near a porticoed window. Sometimes, one finds Mary seated, even upon a throne. This is hardly commensurate with the depiction of a carpenter's wife, of a working class peasant's hut of wattle and daub construction, with a dirt floor. Mary wears no homespun rags. She appears leisured, having been reading, thinking, maybe napping, as opposed to the likelihood that she had little time to herself and was illiterate. The Archangel Gabriel, no less finely garbed, has brought to her a bouquet of radiant lilies. A dove descends to the open window. In Federico Barocci's oil[10] from 1592-96, a cat naps upon a pillow in the foreground. Did Jesus know this cat while growing up? I believe he did. I believe that Jesus, even, was a cat person.

Φέρειν νίκη transliterated: "Veronica"; translated: "true image," from the Latin *vera* for true, ica from the Greek *eikon*, or our modern *icon*. Thus Saint Veronica is a historical flub in that, as the sixth Station of the Cross shows us a woman, a Veronica, wiping the face of Jesus, the word "veronica" itself refers to the image of Jesus' face miraculously left on the woman's cloth, and not the woman who showed charity. The Gospels make no mention of this woman wiping Jesus' face during the Passion. This nameless woman's legend gains momentum beginning in the twelfth century. Still, the Vatican possesses a "Veronica" which it displays Passion Sunday, in the fifth week of Lent. Of the Church's many "Holy Faces," most of them smack remarkably of medieval representations of the human face in artistic rendering. Myth making art making myth is legend is religion.

A modernized Archangel Gabriel serves as the main character of Salman Rushdie's *Satanic Verses*.

---

10   http://en.wikipedia.org/wiki/File:Barocci_Annunciation.jpg

Yet another bear ransacked the cabin, as one did when the neighbor wrote of the bear in the kitchen. I learned about this, the new bear, from Mom on a trip into town where the cell phone worked. The cabin sits in Squaw Valley, in the Sierra Nevada Mountains, far from any mission. I told Mom of the bears in the mountains of north Georgia. She told me to be careful while jogging. Afterwards, I was even more nervous about bears. Thanks Mom. The bear that broke into the cabin ate the microwave.

When supplies dwindled in San Diego, Monterey, San Antonio, and San Gabriel, the priests, soldiers, and neophytres resorted to surviving off the milk of their cows. Finally, a ship from San Blas, leveled almost to the ocean's surface with flour, beans, and beloved chocolate, sailed into San Diego Bay, saving the mission and presidio. Contrary winds kept the vessel from continuing north for a rescue. Father Serra remembered that south of San Antonio sat the valley that Father Juan Crespí and Captain Portolá had explored in 1769, where they found deep holes dug into the valley floor. And he remembered that the exploring party soon discovered the mysterious holes' cause was grizzly bears, digging for roots. They thus named it El Valle de Los Osos, the Valley of the Bears. And in this famine Father Serra ordered up a hunting party. Afterwards, when the soldiers returned to San Antonio and Monterey, they'd netted over 9,000 pounds of dried bear meat, along with seeds for which they had traded from the Chumash that lived in the vicinity. The natives were awed by the power with which the Europeans' guns took down the massive creatures, and Father Serra knew that he would soon take down the Devil, too, by founding his Mission of San Luis

Obispo de Tolosa in El Valle de Los Osos, and converting the heathen there to God.

While on the three-month voyage from Cadiz, Spain, to Vera Cruz, Nueva España, his shipmates wondered why he did not complain of the thirst that all suffered due to their mere cup-a-day ration of water. Father Serra explained: talk little and eat less, and so retain your saliva.

"In times of hunger, there was almost always enough milk available to the inhabitants of the missions, and the Franciscan friars encouraged, and even forced, their neophytes to drink it. However, while humans are among the only mammals capable of drinking milk into and through adulthood, not all have this ability. Europeans are among the few ethnicities with the correct enzymes to digest milk; the indigenous people of the Americas, for the most part, are unable to digest milk past infancy, which actually contributed to the dysentery and even the death of some converts in the missions." From Shipek, "The Conflict Between the California Indian and White Civilization," p. 184.

While in the YMCA Indian Guides, my Chumash Tribe met weekly in rotation at a boy's and his family's home. While at each boy's home that boy's father was "chief" for the night. We had a ridiculous leather drum, and a "chief's headdress" that was so Hollywood costume it could've come from *The Seven Cities of Gold*, or some equally horrendous Indian movie. One boy's father got so into this role that he wore a stoic look and spoke in mono and disyllabic broken English for the night: "Little Big Stick will smack-em drum for all tribe to hear." My father's eyes lit as he failed to keep down a cackle. That guy—this boy's father who made these jokes—like my father, suffered a stroke. That boy's father talks no longer, not in any syllables. My father continued, for years, to laugh loudly at his and others' jokes, until his own stroke consumed him, and, at the time that I wrote this, he could stand only small crowds without being overwhelmed. And still, today, he sometimes chuckles, though he hardly ever laughs, not like he used to, not with that fire in his eyes.

The Chumash of El Valle de Los Osos called themselves the Stishni, separating themselves from Chumash of other regions, those varying tribes of the central California coast that spoke mutually unintelligible dialects of their Hokan language. This made learning their languages impossible for the Spanish friars, to say nothing of translating the Doctrina. Thus the priests baptized few natives, despite the help that the tribes offered the fledgling settlements in the form of meat and acorn meal, which the Spaniards found repugnant. Some from these cultures, feeling threatened by the newcomers, shot flaming arrows into the thatched roofs of the mission structures. And why wouldn't they feel threatened when priests chastised them for performing, for example, their Coyote Dance, wherein a man donned a coyote-skin-and-skull costume and danced, while a singer sang his tale, which lamented the human feces strewn about the Earth. Coyote, meantime, tried to get an onlooker to lick his genitals, and finally engaged in public sexual intercourse with a female tribe member or two, then Coyote ended the dance by defecating. Though the Franciscans called such forbidden acts *devilry*, the Chumash continued their Datura-based religion, along with the enforced Christianity. For the Chumash, the Earth was made of two enormous snakes that caused earthquakes when they slithered past one another—a vast reptilian tectonics. In the 20th century, long after Junípero Serra and his cohorts had died, when asked by an anthropologist about religious contradictions, conflating the Datura and Christian cults, a Chumash man replied, incredulous: "But these are two *different* religions."

The Chumash Indians were a matriarchal society. It's clear why the Spanish understood so little of them. The Chumash were an advanced civilization, constructing sea-worthy canoes called *Tomol* from redwood sanded with sharkskin, the planks caulked with pine resin and naturally occurring tar that washed ashore from the oil wells that now, off the coast of California, are platformed for our consumption. The Spaniards in their anthropocentrism could not conceive of a society more civilized than their own.

Prior to writing this I had been to San Luis Obispo once, up on the Coast Starlight from L.A., one rain-doused morning. I began my first reading of *The Sound and the Fury* and could not get past Benjy's section. Years later I understood what was happening—some synapses finally firing—and I read till the end, when Dilsey takes Benjy to the Black church on Easter Sunday, and afterwards Luster drives Benjy to the boneyard and takes that wrong turn and the man-child howls and howls.

I returned to San Luis Obispo on a book tour. Trapped there—or near there—at Avila Beach, the result of a tsunami thrashing Japan and its waves coursing the Pacific to rabble the California coast. I awoke to watch this from a cliff swathed in iceplant and California brome. Nothing happened. But not some seven thousand miles away in Japan. Houses ripped open and floated like cardboard. In California the tide came in—a surge—rose swiftly, then dissipated. That was all. In SLO I ate breakfast at Luisa's. It would not be until sometime later that I saw footage of the tsunami in Japan and thought about its impact and thought about humans and babies and old people and everyone left trying to pick up and live, and then sometimes I might cry.

In 7th and 8th grades at Gambetta School in Castroville, some Mexican kids wore cross necklaces tatted from waxed thread. These looped and intricate two-toned crosses—red and black, usually—these kids learned to make in juvenile hall. The Norteños were a street gang in Castroville and some of the gang members' kids were quickly working their way to full membership. This kid I knew, Tony Hernandez, already had tattoos. I mean, we were in the 7th grade. I watched him kill a puppy once. The poor thing had wandered onto the school's field during recess and Tony caught it by the scruff and twirled around with his arm outstretched, like he gripped a furry discus, and he tossed the puppy over a fence into the artichoke fields. The dog gave out a short sharp yelp, and we heard nothing more. Tony made shivs from concrete nails that he'd flattened when a train passed over them on the railroad tracks, and which he then sharpened razor sharp. Tony gave me one of these red and black (red was the Norteño color) tatted crosses, but now I don't know what happened to it. I do know what happened to Tony: after he dropped out in our freshman year of high school, he went to a party and was shot and stabbed, and he died.

Imagine your parents not parenting you at all, not sending you to school, not caring if you went to jail, or even if you ate. That's what I imagined it was like for Tony, for other children of gang member parents in Castroville. And that's how life was for Saint Louis, Bishop of Toulouse, for whom Mission San Luis Obispo, and the later city in California, was named. Louis's father, Charles II, Charles the lame, king of Naples and Albania, gave up his child as a hostage in his release from captivity by Peter III of Aragon during the Rebellion of the Sicilian Vespers. Consequently, Louis's gang became the Franciscans in Spain, as opposed to the royal gang that he might have joined. He was thus consecrated bishop of Toulouse by Pope Boniface VIII. He died in 1297.

After Father Serra prayed a novena for San José's intercession, and lo, a lookout sighted the *San Antonio*'s sails come to rescue the starving Spaniards—what seemed to the priest a miracle—Europeans would stay in California, and Blessed Father Fray Junípero Serra would reap a great harvest of souls. By the end of mission secularization in 1836—sixty-six years after the *San Antonio* rescued the Spaniards—Native American populations in California had declined by seventy-three percent.[11]

With the bear hunt of 1772 in El Valle de Los Osos thus began the extirpation of grizzly bears in what would eventually become the contiguous United Stated States of America.

In the later years of Spanish colonial California, vaqueros lassoed grizzlies and dragged them groaning down a pueblo's main drag. In the rodeo they tied bears paw-to-hoof to bulls,

---

11   See Cook, Sherburne F.

then clubbed, whipped, yelled at, and smacked both animals toward one the other, forcing them to fight, till one or both of them died. Few bulls could manage a California grizzly. The beasts reared on their hind legs, towered near ten feet high, and swapped down a terrible clawed paw that easily broke a bull's neck. Whatever animal was left standing, bloodied and panting—already scared nearly enough to death—was shot.

A grizzly bear flies prominently on the "Bear Flag" of the state of California, though the last known California grizzly was shot in 1922.

The last Mexican Governor of California, Rio de Jesus Pico, was a third generation Californian. His paternal grandfather, Santiago de la Cruz Pico, came from Arizona with Juan Bautista de Anza in 1776.

My fucking computer crashed. But I wouldn't stop, and I longhanded during the rest of my stay in the mountains.

Mission San Luis Obispo was the first to erect kilns for firing tiles that roofed the buildings. The leaders of Indian insurrections against the mission in its first year (flaming arrows, thatched roofs), were sent to Monterey as prisoners. Father Serra unsuccessfully tried daily to convert the men through baptism to Catholicism. One of the men was found swinging by the neck from the Presidio rafters when the venerable prelate appeared yet again to coerce his soul to salvation.

After raising the foundation cross and celebrating High Mass, Blessed Father Fray Junípero Serra left Father José

Cavaller in charge of the two neophytes from Monterey he had been allotted. The Blessed Father *presidente* continued south to San Gabriel, from whence he would lead the supply train from San Diego north to Monterey. Cavaller and his neophytes, along with the five-man *escalta* of *soldados de cuera*, set to work constructing the first of Mission San Luis Obispo's buildings: the chapel and priest's quarters. As when describing all the other missions, Father Francisco Palou writes of the Natives' happiness at setting to work for the father. No mention is ever made of houses to be built for the Indians.

The native neophytes forced to work erecting and maintaining mission buildings, grounds, and fields, did so with wooden, bone, and stone tools. Alta California's remote location (1,800 miles from San Blas, Nyarit, New Spain's closest port) made the importation of modern tools difficult.

Father Serra wrote, complaining of the slow baptismal pace: "Every few leagues one encounters an entirely different language!" In California, at that time North America's most linguistically-diverse region, the Franciscan attributed his inability to learn the natives' languages to his own sins. He longed for his longtime confessor and companion, Father Francisco Palou, to whom he wrote: "The occasion might arise in which we could personally embrace each other." But Serra wrote only that he'd leave to Palou's imagination the joy that such an embrace would inspire in their breasts.

My friend Randy and I became friends in our freshman year of high school, when we had sleepovers and started shooting guns. Randy was already impatient with his church, where his mother played the organ. He was not a Catholic, and I sometimes asked him what religion he practiced. He always said, "Just Christian." Neither of us knew what a Protestant was. During my Confirmation, when I asked Father Scott about different church denominations, he said, "There are many ways to love God." Sometimes, during a Saturday sleepover, I'd ask Randy if he wanted to go to church with my family and me on Sunday morning, and Randy always said no.

In 1772, while traveling south from Monterey, when Father Serra came to the hill that looks across the sloping plain that runs from the foot of the San Gabriel Mountains to the ocean, he was pleased with the choice for the mission's site. He foresaw that that land could sustain a large city. Within a few years, the Spanish Crown, eager to colonize California and so protect its claims against the incursions of the Russians and English, would establish in this plain El Pueblo de Nuestra Señora la Reina de Los Angeles del Río Porciuncula.

Blessed Father Fray Junípero Serra had a long history of insolence when it came to secular authority. He famously never got along with any of the military commanders of Nueva California, especially Don Pedro Fages Beleta. The friar's allies included Visitador General Don José de Galvez y Gallardo, marquéz de Sonora, and Viceroy of New Spain Antonio María de Bucareli y Ursua, marquéz de Valleheresa y conde de Jerera. While, in truth, the Spanish expansion into Alta California came under the threat of Russian annexation, the crown knew that the best way to affect the colonization was to enlist the Franciscans and their zealous leader in the conversion of the extant native tribes and thus bring them into the fold of the empire through religion. Pedro Fages, strained by his station's remote location and lack of soldiers, chafed under the *padre presidente's* ambitions to found more missions, and could not supply the *soldados de cuera*. And so, Father Serra's mission south for the supplies for the northern missions did not end there; he would continue on to Mexico City seeking the viceroy's support.

Don Pedro Fages Beleta, governor of colonial California (1770 – 1774 and 1782 – 1791) was nicknamed El Oso, the Bear. He makes a brief fictional appearance in Isabel Allende's novel *Zorro*[12], where he constantly feuds with his rich wife, Eulalia. In real life The Bear fought for control over Upper California against Father Junípero Serra.

Have I said that I am a liar? Let it be known: I am a liar.

After I'd quit drinking I again ran up the mountain, and at its rounded top I found a Toyota. Inside sat a bear, and in the passenger seat Zorro gripped the end of the lasso with which he'd lassoed his bear to the steering wheel. Jimi

---

12   Zorro is a fictional character created by Johnston McCulley in his 1919 novella *The Curse of Capistrano*. Among the handful of potential inspirations for the character of Zorro is Tiburcio Vazquez, an "outlaw" who claimed himself as a defender of Mexican-American rights against the *norteamericanos* that had invaded what would become the state of California. Vazquez's great great grandfather came to California from Sonora Mexico in 1776, with the colonists led by Juan Bautista de Anza.

Hendrix's cover of Dylan's "Like a Rolling Stone" blared from the dash. They passed a joint, Zorro and his bear. I jogged back down the mountain, wanting to 1) not sweat in the Toyota's back seat; and 2) have nothing to do with any of that scene.

The Scriptural Way of the Cross provides no stations for devotion to any falling by Jesus in his sojourn. Most of the details of the fourteen Stations of the Cross that I grew up with—as set by Pope Clement XII in 1731—are not mentioned in any of the Gospels. Who came up with this story of Jesus falling three times? By his second fall, Jesus' knees are scuffed open and bloody. The soldiers stand ready to whip him, to prod his body with the blunt spear-end. Save one: a solitary soldier offers a hand and arm under an arm. Who is this compassionate Roman? Would he buy me a beer? Will you emulate him, this man who helps a man to die?

In 1772 Father Serra, while returning to Mexico City, brought along with him a companion, an Indian boy of no more than twelve years, one among the first converts at Monterey, a boy with soft brown skin. The priest was then fifty-nine years old. I imagine that when both the mission *presidente* and his former gentile charge fell sick with typhus, the friar cared nothing for himself and tended, sweating and delirious, calling the boy *¡mi hijo!*, and bringing a bowl of cold spring water to the boy's cotside.

Scott O'Dell's 1960 children's novel *Island of the Blue Dolphins* is based on the story of a lone Indian woman left on the island of San Nicolas, of the Santa Barbara Channel

Islands, off the California coast. She was "rescued" in an effort sponsored by the missions, but upon reaching the mainland she died within seven weeks. Her name, given to her by Father Gonzales of Mission Santa Barbara upon her deathbed baptism, was Juana María.

In *Island of the Blue Dolphins*, the protagonist is left alone on her island after her remaining tribespeople—survivors to a brutal Aleut slaying—board a mainland-bound barque. Among famous Aleuts is Cungagnaq, or Saint Peter the Aleut, a martyr of the Russian Orthodox Church who was tortured and murdered by Catholic California missionaries at San Francisco de Asís, commonly known as Mission Dolores, mission of sorrows, mission of pain.

When Peter the Aleut would not renounce his Eastern Orthodox faith the padre of San Francisco had a toe severed from each foot with each refusal, totaling ten. The native Ohlones employed in this gruesome task—their obsidian chiseled knives slicing through skin and chopping through bone—continued as per their orders, and cut off as well each of Peter's fingers. They quartered the martyr, spilled his bowels, as if from bear attack, attack by a bear in the shape of a Catholic.

Where Did I Come From? My parents bought this book and read it to us. Other than the *Joy of Sex* incident, I don't remember my parents ever having "the talk" with me. No priest ever told me that masturbation was a mortal sin. My first orgasm came while masturbating, although it's doubtful I knew that's what I was doing. It simply felt good to touch myself. I was in the shower. An alien rushing overcame me. It wasn't sticky and white, as *Where Did I Come From?* describes it, but mostly clear and viscous. Immediately afterwards I felt nausea. Thinking of girls then was like thinking of eating a cheeseburger when I'd overeaten. Then guilt. These feelings—coupled with the aforementioned guilt—always came on after I masturbated until I was about seventeen years old.

When I was four or five and could not sleep while staying with my grandparents, I walked into their bedroom and found them engaged in the act of mutual masturbation.

Catholic doctrine states: "Every genital act must be within the framework of marriage" and that "the moral sense of the faithful have declared without hesitation that masturbation is an intrinsically and seriously disordered act" because it lacks "the full sense of mutual self-giving and human procreation in the context of true love."[13]

By the time of my sophomore year in high school, in my health class, Mr. Gardner (the mustachioed and balding redhead who also coached girls' softball) taught us that masturbation was a normal—in fact a healthy—part of one's sexuality.

The mission system in California provided for a minimum of two friars per establishment, though in many cases a solitary friar ministered to his flock of *soldados de cuera* until further padres came to the new province. I assume, that in a gentilian frontier far from the Spaniard's concept of "civilization," loneliness and boredom must've necessitated the deviation from standards of behavior, if only to break up the monotony of an otherwise routine day.

---

13   http://www.ewtn.com/library/curia/cdfcertn.htm

Won over by Father Serra's zeal, with his "boy" as evidence of the spiritual fruit to be harvested in California, the Viceroy made provisions to care for the missions, including the expedition of Juan Bautista de Anza overland from Sonora, which would bring settlers. He removed Pedro Fages as military governor, and replaced him with Don Fernando Javier Rivera y Moncada. Don Fernando would later be excommunicated by the padres for forcibly removing from the priests' protection an alleged leader of a native uprising in San Diego.

Among the supplies the viceroy provided for the missions was a coarse sackcloth from which the padres instructed the natives to make clothing for themselves and so cover their nakedness, thus no longer tempting the Spaniards, and inducing shame in the Indians, and so making them "civilized."

Before leaving Mexico City to return to California, and before leaving the College of San Fernando, Father Serra asked for, and was granted, permission to kiss the feet of all the friars present, including the novices. The result of this display of great humility was many tears among his fellow Franciscans.

While I grew up, nakedness, or more often wearing nothing but one's underwear, was not a big deal. Mornings, when I emerged from my bedroom and looked down the hall to the kitchen, my dad stood at the sink readying the coffee wearing nothing but his Jockey shorts. Mom once ran topless out of her bedroom to get the phone while Randy stood in the foyer, dumbfounded. We all still laugh about it. Mom says, "I guess I gave Randy quite a thrill." She pokes Randy in the chest in jest. On my first sleepover at Randy's house I awoke early and couldn't fall back to sleep, so I played this computer game where one flew an F-14 on dogfight sorties. The computer sat in Randy's parents' living room. Randy's mom, fully dressed, hair finished, makeup applied, peeked around a corner to where I played the game in my briefs. She asked if I wanted any breakfast. When Randy finally showed up, likewise fully clothed, his eyebrows squiggled together as he looked me up and down and said, "What are you doing?" I replied, honestly and naïvely enough, "Playing computer."

Jared Diamond's 1998 book *Guns, Germs and Steel: The Fates of Human Societies* attributes global Eurasian socio-political dominance to geographic accidents, hence the jets simulated in pixels in gigabytes in the above-mentioned computer game. These are representations of actual jets developed by the United States military, the United States itself a product of Eurasian colonialism, continuing ongoing colonialism by spreading a military empire across Earth.

Serial killer Albert Fish hit himself repeatedly with a nail-studded paddle, inserted needles into his perineum, and once sequestered himself, all because—according to Fish's own testimony—John the Apostle told him to do so.

Blessed Father Fray Junípero Serra sewed barbs to the inside of his habit so that they would flay his skin throughout the day, a constant reminder of his sins, and his unworthiness before God.

Frederic Wertham, psychiatrist and expert witness during Albert Fish's murder trial, claimed that Fish's religious obsession drove him to child sacrifice in penance for his own sins. Fish's cannibalism, Wertham said, was a form of communion. A witness for the prosecution said that religious cannibalism was a "matter of taste." Fish confessed to the murder and consumption of three children, ages four, five, and ten[14].

When Father Serra returned to Monterey from Mexico City, with "his" Indian "boy" safe, he rejoiced. Had the native died en route the Blessed Father worried that his work converting the Indians might be stalled due to the loss of trust amongst his neophytes. He was overjoyed at the mission's ongoing work under direction of his companion, Father Juan Crespí. And upon this homecoming, the *padre presidente* caressed his Rumsen and Esselen as if they were his own children.

> "[W]as it then, in the glitter of that remote summer, that the rift in my life began; or was my excessive desire for that child only the first evidence of an inherent singularity?"—Humbert Humbert

The Hamptons lived a few doors down on our street, and had children much older than me and my brother and sister. The Hamptons' youngest, Scott, was in high school when I was about six or seven. One day while I was riding my bike Scott beckoned me up his driveway. I didn't know to say no—he was not a complete stranger, although I'd never talked with him before, only seen him in his yard—and I worried what he might do if I said no, that he might stomp down the driveway and beat me up. I think he said he had

---

14   "Fish Held Insane By Three Experts. Defense Alienists Say Budd Girl's Murderer Was And Is Mentally Irresponsible." *New York Times*. May 21, 1935. Retrieved 2011-12-09. "Three psychiatrists testified in Supreme Court today that Albert H. Fish, on trial for the murder of Grace Budd in June, 1928, was legally insane when he committed the murder and has been insane since that date."

something cool to show me. I think it was that much of a cliché, and I was that gullible too, but I'm pretty sure that's what he said. Otherwise I don't know why I would've gone into that house; I'd never been inside before. Scott's father, a Vietnam vet confined to a wheelchair, sat in his living room watching television and smoking cigarettes when we walked down the hall to Scott's bedroom. Scott closed the door behind us. From under his mattress he withdrew a pornographic magazine. I had not seen many naked women, and the *Joy of Sex* contained illustrations, not photographs. A woman looked seductively over her shoulder, across her mostly bubble-bath-soap-covered body, but with her ass cheeks exposed. Scott said, "You like that?" I don't remember if I responded, but I do remember that this feeling came up in my stomach, a sickness, an intuition that I was somewhere I should not have been. There was something wrong with Scott's voice. He didn't sound like he only wanted to show me something cool; he sounded breathy and quiet, like he had already done some hard physical labor, or was about to. I tried to back my way to the door. Scott said, "You like this, then?" He hadn't turned the page in his magazine. His eyes motioned mine down, where he'd pulled his penis out of his pants. Now I was scared. Scott said, "Get down there and suck my cock." I whimpered that I wanted to go. Scott said, forcefully, "Put it in your mouth." I started crying and Scott's father yelled from the living room, which must've been what turned everything around, because Scott put his dick away, told me that it was okay, then let me out the door, and I ran down the hallway. As I ran I heard Scott's and his father's shouts at each other. I kept running, back through the garage and down the driveway to my bike, and I pedaled home. I did not tell my parents about it then, and did not tell them at all until after I'd grown. I don't know why I never told them when I was little. I suppose somehow I thought that what had happened was something shameful and something that should be kept private. Two years after that incident, Scott Hampton stole my bicycle, and we learned this because I discovered one of my own friends riding his bike with my mag wheels attached to it, wheels that my friend said he'd bought from Scott Hampton. Dad took me to Scott Hampton's house, and again to that garage, where we found my bicycle in pieces. Scott had to retrieve the parts he'd sold, return the money, and return my bike. Later, as an adult, one night I told my dad about what had happened in Scott's bedroom long ago—and we were a few beers in, my dad's eyes drooping with weariness—all Dad said was, "That Scott Hampton was bad news."

Also down our street lived the Allens and their daughter Claudette, with whom I had some of my first experiences with the opposite sex. She played with me and my brother and sister at our house, in our yard. I remember thinking that she was a *dirty* girl because of her name; it sounded like the dirt clods—Claudette—that we threw at each other during our backyard battles. She was also a brunette with piercing black eyes. I hadn't then any knowledge of Shakespeare's dark lady, but if I did, that's who I'd associate Claudette with. My brother was a towhead who could've blinded you, and my sister and I were both dirty blondes, dirty like Claudette. Dad had constructed a playhouse, enclosed with a wooden door, complete with glass windows and drapes. Behind that playhouse I watched Claudette drop her pants, squat, and leave a turd curled and collecting flies in the dirt. Inside the playhouse we played doctor. This was all innocent I'll-show-you-mine-you-show-me-yours kind of stuff.

There were two little girls, sisters, who lived down the street, blondes, about a year apart. The older might've had a year on me. We played, often getting naked in the playhouse where we'd set up a reclining lawn chair and a table, so that it resembled an actual house. When Dad built the playhouse I tossed him shingles from the ground up to the rafters where he nailed them in place. At least I'd like to think I did that, but in reality, he was likely only making me feel like I helped because I was too little to help anyone, even myself, because I was fucking five years old or something. The older sister was my first kiss. My recollection of her tongue was that it was slimy, a little salty. We stood under oaks, amidst California brome, the seed pods of which stuck in our socks and itched our calves. In the finished playhouse we undressed and examined one another. Those little girls pulled open the labia of their vaginas so I could see their pink insides. Once, the King boy was babysitting and he peered through the wood-slatted walls and yelled, "I can see you in there and I'm going to tell your parents." Another time, the younger girl—when we were all three of us naked—lay on the lawn chair and instructed me to lie on top of her. She spread her legs. I did not have an erection that I can remember. This little girl pulled me toward her by my penis and told me to put it inside of her. I said no, that that looked like it would hurt. She said, "It feels good." I don't know what happened to those sisters, because the family moved away. As I remembered this, wrote it down, and told my wife about it, her eyes widened and she said, "Something was definitely wrong for those little girls. That's way too much information for a little girl to know."

In my seventh or eighth grade year, neighbor girls came to play with my sister, their little breasts budding. We play-wrestled upon Mom's bed, where I copped feels. They never said anything, but I worried. Was I those little girls' Scott Hampton?

By 1775 Fathers Luis Jayme and Vicente Fuster had moved Mission San Diego from its original site near the presidio to about six miles upriver, in order not to taint their neophyte charges by proximity to the licentious soldiers. On October 3, 1775, sixty native Kumeyaay were baptized alone, and the padres rejoiced in the spiritual harvest they were reaping out of this vineyard of the Lord.

Father Serra absolutely believed that the slow rate of conversion of the native people was due to the influence of the Devil, who had been outraged by the coming of the Catholics to California, this region that he had long held in his dominion.

While the Devil is never physically described in the Old or New Testaments, in medieval texts such as the Codex Gigas from the thirteenth century, he is depicted variously as having animal body parts, faces where his elbows, knees, and ass would be, and covered with sores or scars and hair. He often carries a pitchfork and has a tail. Today, many Christians still believe in this cartoonish persona. Some high-ranking priests in the Curia of the Catholic Church, for example, see the Devil in the work of J.K. Rowling, and her books centered on her character of Harry Potter, despite the obvious Christian allegory. I mean, Harry sacrifices himself for those he loves and he comes back to life and all. See the previous paragraphs about *Turner and Hooch*.

It got *cold*. I wore sweatpants while running and burned fires in the fireplace. My studio reeked of woodfire. If I caught a bear, his skewered parts would've sizzled in that fireplace.

What I mean is: Harry Potter sacrifices himself for his friends because he loves them, not unlike Hooch sacrificing himself for Turner, or Jesus sacrificing himself for all humanity (if you subscribe to such a belief). And this thing, this "love," it seems to last beyond the individual.

Of the recent converts in San Diego, two men left the mission grounds to recruit six hundred Kumeyaay for an attack. The army descended into the San Diego River valley and split into two groups: one to attack the mission, the other the presidio. When the pagans reached the Indian *reducciones*, they forbade the converts from calling out to alert the mission guards. Then they set fire to the wattle and daub and thatched roof buildings. Waking to the smell of smoke, Father Luis Jayme approached the Kumeyaay raiding the mission complex, a pale palm to the air, shouting, "*¡Amar a dios, hijos!*" The natives surrounded the priest then closed in. They stripped him naked and shot sixteen arrows into his abdomen. They beat his head and face with clubs and boulders, and they dragged his body into a dry arroyo where it was found the next morning, after the fighting had subsided.

When Blessed Father Fray Junípero Serra founded Mission San Diego de Alcalá in 1769, he did so on the site of a Kumeyaay village. Spaniards cut trees to build the mission structures, and their cattle, mules, and horses foraged on land the natives control-burned to kill weeds and grow edible foods, which the European livestock devoured. When Indians captured or killed this livestock, the natives were caught and punished for theft or destruction of property. The *soldados de cuera* rode down Kumeyaay women and raped them.

Camping in Arroyo Seco, not far from Mission Nuestra Señora de la Soledad, while drunk, I stood upon a boulder ringing the fire. The Evan Williams passed. I said, "They're coming for you, and they've got everything, your Social Security number, credit cards, address. We're all fucked." After my swig I fell face forward into yet another boulder, the way one falls into the blue Pacific on a summer day. I lied at work come Monday, and said, "Mountain biking accident." Everyone laughed, asked, "How drunk were you?" Arroyo Seco means "dry creek."

The Kumeyaay scattered when the mission *escolta* gathered, loaded muskets, and fired into the thicket of brown skin glistening in the firelight. Bodies fell. Natives whooped war whoops. This could've happened in Hollywood, one hundred miles north and 170 years later, but it was in what would become San Diego. When the *soldados de cuera* and Father Vicente Fuster found the body of Father Luis Jayme dumped in the arroyo, they knew it was him only by the few patches of white skin showing through where blood had not dried.

Father Palou writes that the only part of Father Jayme's body left untouched by his heathen murderers were his "consecrated hands." Palou says that this was to show that the priest had not committed any evils, and so had died with clean hands.

The Sacraments of Confirmation and Holy Orders are performed by Bishops and include the *laying on of hands*. I was confirmed in 1993 at fifteen years old in the Monterey Diocese by Bishop Sylvester Ryan at Our Lady of Refuge, where the bishop laid his hands on me, bestowing my apostolic name of Matthew.

To separate themselves from the native neophytes, Spaniards, criollos, and mestizos in California referred to themselves as *gente de razon*, or, people of reason.

It was because of Alta California's remote location that Pope Clement XIV granted confirmation powers on Father Serra for that ten-year period.

Franciscans in literature: Friar Tuck of the Robin Hood legend does not appear in original allusions to Robyn Hode, but plays a part in an extant fragment, a play from 1475: *Robin Hood and the Knight*. Friar Tuck challenges Robin to a contest of wits. The wager: who will carry whom across a river. Tuck ends up tossing Robin into the water and becomes one of the Merry Meyne. Popularly, Friar Tuck is depicted as overweight, jovial, and a drunkard.

Piers Plowman.

To see what happens to the survivors of the Spanish, Mexican, and American colonial eras of Alta California, one need only read *Tortilla Flat* by John Steinbeck. Today, Tortilla Flat in Monterey is bisected by the modern Presidio.

As a reward after a doctor or dentist appointment, Mom took me and my brother and sister to the Drive Thru at McDonald's on Del Monte Avenue, and after that, we took our hamburgers and french fries to Dennis the Menace Park, and after lunch I played on the old steam engine locomotive, on the suspension bridge, in the maze, and slid down the long slides that covered the hill overlooking Lake El Estero. In a 1791 drawing by José Cardero, the presidio and chapel of Monterey lie a hundred yards from the shores of Lake El Estero, where the Royal Presidio Chapel still stands. Estero means "estuary," oh metaphor-starved Spanish.

The summary of chapter five from John Steinbeck's *Tortilla Flat*: "How St. Francis turned the tide and put a gentle punishment on Pilon and Pablo and Jesus Maria." These three paisanos get drunk and leave a candle blessed for Saint Francis burning on the table. In the night, the candle's flame lights a calendar, then a loose piece of wallpaper, then a pile of newspapers, then the entire house becomes a candle for Saint Francis. Chapter seven: "How Danny's friends assisted the Pirate to keep a vow, and how as a reward for merit the Pirate's dogs saw a holy vision." Pirate, an old hermit, vows to buy a gold candle for Saint Francis for the saint's intercession in the life of one of Pirate's many dogs. Danny, Pilon, Pablo, Big Joe Portagee, and Jesus Maria bring Pirate's vow to fruition at the Royal Presidio Chapel, where a candle burns before the image of Saint Francis, and Father Ramon tells of the saint's love of animals, and that it is no sin to love the beasts. After church, Pirate preaches to his dogs in a bower of Monterey's pine forest. These dogs Pirate believes to have seen a vision, and he calls them good and lucky Catholic dogs. The recovered dog for which Pirate prayed gets run over by a truck.

In preparation for the Sacred Expedition, lamenting that there was then no plan for a mission in honor of St. Francis, Visitador General José de Gálvez said, "Should God show us his port, let there be established the Mission of San Francisco." In 1769, on their overland expedition from San Diego in search of Monterey Bay, Don Gaspar de Portolá and Father Juan Crespí unknowingly passed over Monterey Bay and from a mountaintop spied what they thought to be a great *mediterraneo*, or inland sea, which they named in honor of San Francisco.

In response to news of the attack on Mission San Diego, and the murder of Father Luis Jayme, Blessed Father Fray Junípero Serra exclaimed, "Thanks be to God! Now surely the Indians of San Diego shall be converted to our Holy Faith!" The Father thought that, in the Church's mercy, the Indians would be drawn to conversion.

When Jesus spoke to the daughters of Jerusalem, he preached for them not to weep for him, but to cry for themselves and their children, for there will come a time when people will proclaim, "Blessed are the barren." How is it that this man who had been arrested, spat upon, yelled at and lied to, punched, flogged with spiked whips, degraded with a crown of thorns and pummeled with a reed scepter, who had already struggled to carry the implement of his death this far, who had already fallen twice and had another, one Simon of Cyrene, forced to help him carry the cross, had the strength to stop, preach to these women loudly enough for someone else to hear and record what he said, without any of the Roman soldiers who thus far have impatiently flogged and prodded him to keep him moving toward execution, and why did he say what he said, and what the hell does it mean? Most remain inconclusive on any interpretation of the eighth Station of the Cross, though Catholics teach their children that sometimes all we think about is ourselves, and look at this example: Jesus stopped in the midst of his agony to preach to ailing women. This makes much sense when reading the scripture, which claims the women wept for him, and Jesus tells the women to weep for themselves, though he was the condemned man, he who had been whipped and ridiculed and pushed to this end, yea, the women ought to weep for themselves. Yet another interpretation is that the Daughters of Jerusalem were a group of Jewish widows who followed the condemned to their executions and made a show of weeping for them. So, it's possible that they didn't know who Jesus was at all.

In a letter to the viceroy concerning the fates of the leaders of the insurrection at San Diego, Father Serra insisted that the arrested pagans be released without punishment. "Through our mercy," he wrote, "shall much fruit be reaped for the Lord." But this letter arrived in Mexico City a week after the viceroy had sent orders for the assailants to be punished. Upon receiving the orders from the viceroy, Governor Rivera y Moncada forcibly removed the neophytes who had organized the attacks from the priest's protection, at sword-point, ignoring the padres' pleading for peace.

Carlos, one of the Kumeyaay neophytes who organized the attack, saw his Franciscan Father's soft hands and knew that he was a man who would not wield a whip and so took solace in his habit and Holy Faith.

A sketch of Governor Rivera y Moncada seizing the frightened Carlos from the Mission Church depicts the Franciscans at a distance, hopeless in the background. The Army Captain looms over the much smaller native who is barefoot and clothed by the coarse cloth the crown had deemed ..itable for Indians. The Fathers pray; sea gulls flit over San Diego Bay. After his release, Carlos would kill again, and neophytes would be caught stockpiling weapons. Junípero Serra recommended life imprisonment for Carlos, so that he might daily be taught the virtues of Christian life. The *presidente* wanted, more than anything, for this savage to die as a child of God. Serra claimed that the Devil's hold on Carlos—as Satan continued to tempt him to fight the Spanish—was proof that the poor Kumeyaay man did not even know his own mind.

I talked to my brother the other night on the phone, and he told me that my niece, who is "definitely starting her terrible twos," knows when she's in trouble because she rolls her eyes in an attempt to break eye contact. But Carlos. Carlos of course did not know his own mind, and could not have wanted the Spanish to go away so that the Kumeyaay way of life prior to European contact might continue as it had before.

In October of 1775, having recruited his colonists from Sinaloa and Sonora, Mexico, Juan Bautista de Anza ordered the party to mount up before leaving Tubac in modern Arizona for the overland trek to Alta California. In about nine months he would land at the site of what would become the mission and presidio of San Francsico de Asís. On his return to Mexico, Anza would survey the area that became the ground for El Pueblo de San José de Guadalupe.

While I tell this story of San Francisco, it is worth mentioning that the October in which I wrote this, while I was stranded in those Georgia mountains, the San Francisco Giants won the National League West and were battling it out for the Division title against the Atlanta Braves.

In Confirmation catechism—and especially during the weeklong retreat prior to Confirmation Sunday during Pentecost—boys and girls were separated for instruction. My sister learned in the basement classrooms at Richard's Hall, from the bespectacled and short cropped, curly-haired Mrs. P, who taught that premarital sex and abortion were sins: *thou shalt not spill thy seed; thou shalt not destroy thy unblessed offspring.* I have no recollection of my Eucharistic Ministers during Confirmation Catechism ever telling me not to sin against chastity. My feeling here, is that the Church taught girls to keep their legs closed, and taught boys to live solely for God. Before the advent of modern cable my parents were lucky to have a television in their bedroom, one with a digital channel readout, unlike the larger analog set that graced our living room. Premium channels—HBO, Showtime—sold by subscription only, were something Dad would never pay for. But, through some godsent twitch in the airwaves, if

I turned the television in my parents' bedroom to digital channel sixteen, out from the snow and static into brief audio and visual clarity for fractions of seconds flashed bits from the Playboy Channel. Glimpses of thighs, a squiggled breast, snatches of intimate dialogue and breathy pleasured moans poured from the set, an elixir. This, of course, was enough for any thirteen-year-old. I used soap and Vaseline and my own hand. And every time, afterwards, came the nausea and the guilt.

On November 11, 1602, Sebastian Vizcaíno sailed into what he named San Diego Bay, for the feast of St. Didacus was nigh. The men built a hut and the Carmelite friars sang mass. The Kumeyaay Indians paid a visit, geared for war. Vizcaíno reports encountering an old woman who approached with tears streaming her cheeks. Perhaps she foresaw the continued arrival of these pale men and their big ships, and the destruction of her culture. Perhaps she had been told of the white men who had come sixty years earlier. Maybe she had even been there, just a little girl, when Juan Rodriguez Cabrillo had offered his clay beads as if he was a god.

In 1602, when Sebastián Vizcaíno and his friars sang mass on Catalina Island, as many as a hundred Pimugnans witnessed the rite, asking by signs what it was about. According to Vizcaíno's records, the Californians marveled not a little at the idea of Heaven and at the image of Jesus crucified. Vizcaíno was brought to a prairie on Santa Catalina Island where the Pimugnans worshipped their sun god. Upon the prairie they had placed an icon, a headless figure with horns protruding from the body, a figure that Vizcaíno predictably described as a demon. The Pimugnans urged

Vizcaíno not to approach the image of their deity, but he ignored them. He placed his crucifix against the wooden figurine and prayed the Our Father. Vizcaíno told the natives that his prayer was from Heaven, and that their god was the Devil. Vizcaíno held out his crucifix, encouraging the Pimugnans to touch it and receive Jesus. He pointed at the sky and indicated Heaven. The Pimugnans worshipped a sun deity, so they were impressed with this white man and his description of his god, for their gods seemed to be one and the same. It's no wonder then that Vizcaíno's diary reports the natives being pleased with this exchange. "Surely," the diary says, "they will be converted to our Holy Faith."

When Blessed Father Fray Junípero Serra and his fellow Franciscans began their attempt at converting the natives of Alta California, they did so through the forced learning of Spanish. When their earliest converts had gained fluency enough for conversation, they began to tell the fathers stories of bearded men bearing crosses who had appeared before their ancestors. They also described the beautiful woman in blue who spoke their native languages, and who told them to go to the white men, and to not be afraid. Surely, the tribes of California maintained an oral history of their first encounters with Europeans such as Cabrillo and Vizcaíno. But Father Serra saw only divine guidance, and the Devil's influence working against the Franciscans' arrival in Alta California, and the *presidente* worked the Doctrina and the flog to beat the Holy Faith into his new charges.

Throughout European history in California, Spaniards sailed up the Santa Barbara Channel, and Tongva and Chumash Indians rowed out in their plank canoes to the large ships, encouraging the men to come ashore, where there was fresh food and water, for the natives wanted the glass beads they knew the white men carried. Fearing attack, cannibalism, or loss of a rare good northerly wind, the ships continued on past Point Concepcion, to Monterey, where many men were lost to scurvy. Had the Spaniards landed and traded with the natives for fresh fruits and vegetables, many men might have been saved, and California Native Americans' sad history might have been written differently.

When Vizcaíno landed at Monterey Bay, of the men not already dead, forty were too ill to continue, including the pilot, two helmsmen, the cosmographer and the scrivener. The local Rumsen told the Europeans of the acorns that were the staple of their diet. There can be up to sixty milligrams of Vitamin C in one hundred grams of acorn. But the Spanish would not eat this heathenish food that would have saved their lives.

Vizcaíno described Monterey Bay as exactly what his Majesty and his Royal Navy searched for: a perfect harbor for sheltering the Manila Galleons on their long return to Nueva España from the Philippines. Vizcaíno exaggerated the harbor's shelter in his reports, for it lies open to severe northerly driven weather. Because of this, Portolá would miss Monterey on his overland voyage north.

Upon exploring the interior at Monterey Bay, Vizcaíno and his men found and named in honor of Our Lady of Mount Carmel, the river and valley that today bear that name. In the river the men discovered elk with horns, he wrote, more than three yards high. Today, no elk lap the waters at Carmel River. Wineries, golf courses, luxury sedans, and sports cars wind through the valley instead. And at the valley's mouth sits Mission San Carlos Borromeo del Rio Carmelo, under which lie the remains of Blessed Father Fray Junípero Serra. The chaplain's journal aboard Sir Francis Drake's *Golden Hind* during his circumnavigation of 1577-80 speaks of encountering Coast Miwok Indians in California in 1579, when Drake landed in what is today Drake's Bay, north of San Francisco, near Point Reyes. In return for the clothing the English offered to the naked natives, the Miwok brought what the chaplain recorded as *Toba'h*, an herb that could have been tobacco. Within a few days Californians from other tribes arrived to see the newcomers. Drake's chaplain writes that the Indians perceived the white men as gods.

In 1987 a replica of the *Golden Hind* toured California and docked in Moss Landing, where my fifth grade class visited on a field trip. Below deck the quarters looked cozy, the kind of place where I'd like to curl up in a storm-tossed sea, but Mrs. Smith, our teacher, said that that place in a ship would've been like hell because it would've been dark and wet and it would've smelled like the sea and the living things from the sea that had died in it.

The Miwok women wailed and scratched at their faces when their men consorted with Sir Francis Drake and the other Englishmen who had landed on California's coast in the summer of 1579. "The blood streaming downe along their brests, besides despoiling the upper parts of their bodies of those single coverings . . .they would with furie cast themselves upon the ground . . . on hard stones, knobby hillocks, stocks of wood, and pricking bushes." Drake and his men fell themselves to their knees in prayer, their eyes Heavenward, so that the natives might see they prayed to God and they too might worship God then their eyes that had been so blinded by the deceiver might be opened.

Although Hernando de Alarcón's ascent of the Colorado River Delta in 1540 proved that Baja California was a peninsula, Spanish rhetoric written by Father Fray Antonio de la Ascención, Carmelite friar for Vizcaíno's expedition of 1602-3, described Isla California, meant to discredit Sir Francis Drake's claim of Nova Albion for the British monarch. The question of California's connection to North America would not be definite until Don Juan Bautista de Anza's first overland expedition from Sonora to San Francisco in 1774.

Father Fray Antonio de la Ascención writes that the Indians of California can "easily and with very little labor be taught our Holy Catholic faith, and that they would receive it well and lovingly." He calls for two hundred older and honorable soldiers to ensure brotherhood during the conquest, so that peace and love—the best tools to pacify pagans—should reign. The religious, the friar says, should likewise be wise and loving to easily quell animosities between Spaniards and the heathen, and therefore avoid war. The Spaniards should bring with them trinkets—beads, mirrors, knives—to distribute among the gentiles, so that they might come to love the Christians, and see "that they are coming to their lands to give them that of which they bring, and not to take away the Indians' possessions, and may understand that they are seeking the good of their souls." No women are to accompany the conquest, says Father Antonio, "to avoid offenses to God."

When the Sacred Expedition began in 1769 it consisted of three vessels and two overland parties consisting in all of 310 Spaniards, of which 126 survived to reach San Diego. Zero women accompanied the party.

From Father Serra's point of view, his majesty Carlos III of Spain authorized his excellency, Viceroy Antonio María de Bucareli y Ursúa, to explore the Pacific Northwest and in the process establish a mission and presidio on the peninsula at the bay of San Francisco, not because of mounting international pressure against Spain's frontier by Russian and British explorers, but because the royal Catholic monarch in his zeal could not stand the thought of more heathen tribes suffering in Satan's grasp with the Franciscans so near and able to help through conversion.

Father Serra took advantage of an extra padre at San Carlos and sent Father Fermín Lasuén with a small *escalta* of *soldados de cuera* to found Mission San Juan Capistrano between Missions San Gabriel Arcángel and San Diego de Alcalá, at the sight of the Sajavit village of Acjachemen Indians. In a bower of oaks a mile from the cliffs that fell to the sea, the padre had the foundation cross erected and the bells hung. He celebrated High Mass and consecrated the ground for the mission. The *soldados* set to felling trees for the chapel. Before much work could be completed, word about the insurrection at San Diego reached the small party. The *soldados* buried the mission bells and saddled, bringing Father Lasuén with them to the Presidio in San Diego to aid in the rescue of California's first European establishment.

Saint John of Capistrano was an Inquisitor, a Franciscan, an Italian, a Crusades-era military commander against the Turks in Hungary; he ranted against Jews in sermons, prompted Jewish expulsions, oversaw the burning of Jews at the stake at Breslau, died of bubonic plague while fighting Muslims, and was not really an all-around good guy. During WWII, Breslau Jews were herded up and "liquidated." It is safe to say that Breslau does not have a strong pro-Jew history. Nevertheless, despite John's history, and of course long before the further atrocities at Breslau, Father Serra named for San Juan his mission that still sits—almost completely demolished by an earthquake—between San Diego and San Gabriel, California.

In the expanded Star Wars universe the agents of Inquisitorious hunted Jedi who were exterminated like European Jews. Oh gods of originality rain down a deluge of pain.

The channel of El Rio de Nuestra Señora La Reina de Los Angeles de Porciuncula, or the Los Angeles River, is today nearly all concrete. Only a few miles of riverbed remain natural over its forty-three mile course to Long Beach. It was channelized for flood control after the flash flood of 1938 killed 115 people and caused over forty million dollars in damage. The flat swath of land sloping to the Pacific that Father Serra foresaw containing a magnificent city, is in fact an alluvial floodplain.

Collectively, the Ohlone Indians inhabited the central California coast from the San Francisco peninsula and the East Bay to the southern reaches of the Salinas Valley. The tribe broke into distinct regional dialects, with the Ramaytush speakers inhabiting the San Francisco area, a people who called themselves the Yelamu. The Spanish language that was enforced upon them killed their native tongue, while syphilis and measles killed the people themselves.

My grandfather sometimes sang "I Left My Heart in San Francisco" while he fixed his Datsun pickup or tilled his petite syrah. In the early summer of 1776 Father Francisco Palou, along with an *escalta* and Father Pedro Font and Juan Bautista de Anza, set out for the peninsula of the great bay of San Francisco, and there, on the Friday of Sorrows, they found the creek and lagoon that they named appropriately for La Nuestra Señora de Los Dolores. Palou founded Mission San Francisco de Asís, and to this day the mission is nicknamed Dolores.

By the time it came down to game three of the NLCS with the San Francisco Giants against the Philadelphia Phillies, I imagined that if I were home in Atlanta, my wife would not want to talk to me, since she's from Philly and I couldn't help myself but root for the Giants as they worked their way toward the World Series.

Jesus fell a third and final time in his Passion, as depicted in the ninth Station of the Cross. By now it's amazing that this man has made it this far—to the base of Calvary. Bones and rotting garbage and bodies lay strewn about the path that led to the hilltop, refuse from previous executions. Jesus can hardly make it, though Simon of Cyrene encourages him, hefting his cross, the man of the original Blues. The crowd leers round the two. If at first you don't succeed, try again again again. And again, Jesus forces his body up. He stumbles up the hill, as the tradition since the 6th century is that Calvary was a hill, though no one really knows.

Whenever I hear Scott McKenzie's "San Francisco (Be Sure to Wear Flowers in Your Hair)" I think of my grandparents. The song was released in 1967, when my mom was nineteen years old and living in Los Altos, where she had moved with my grandparents from New York in 1951.

When Father Serra himself re-founded Mission San Juan Capistrano, the soldiers and neophytes dug up the buried bells from the founding's first attempt, and, when rung, it's said the Indians came in droves to hear the High Mass sung.

Mission San Juan Capistrano is in Orange County, California, the setting of a ridiculous program called *The O.C.* that ran on the Fox Network from 2003-2007, a show about privileged white high schoolers who endure relationship drama while at the beach.

There was also a movie called *Orange County* wherein some kid applies to Stanford because he read a fictitious novelist's book, one Marcus Skinner, who has fake Rate My Professor and Goodreads pages.

Upon leaving what was not yet at that time Orange County, California, Father Serra and his neophyte companion spent six months traveling north to Monterey. Along the way, the *presidente* spent months at each of his missions, confirming neophytes. In the vast wildernesses between missions the father and his charge curled up fireside, their mules munching the California brome, hides flame-glowing, heat on all of them huddled, a bundle of bodies.

Shortly after departing from Mission San Juan Capistrano, Blessed Father Fray Junípero Serra and his boy were accosted by a band of Acjachemen, all painted with war paint and sprouting from the chaparral with shrieks, fitting arrows into their bows. The padre's neophyte called out to the Indians in their common language and said that if they attacked, a large group of soldiers coming from the south would destroy them with their guns. Although this was a lie, after this speech it is said that the Acjachemen became "gentle as lambs," and the Franciscan made over them the sign of the cross, offered them beads, and the parties departed as friends. The promise was made that this band of Acjachemen would eventually come to the mission. It was not part of the promise that they would later perish from disease.

To see the Golden Gate from the Pacific requires a fogless day, a rarity. Hence no previous explorer, not Cabrillo, Vizcaíno, nor Drake, saw it. Even on a clear day, distant Angel Island fills the view into the bay, making the channel appear shallower than it actually is.

Halloween Day 1769: air quality exceptionally good, clarity unheard of in today's Bay Area. From Twin Peaks the Portolá expedition viewed the tip of the San Francisco peninsula. At sea they spied *Los Farallones*, whitened with sea gull droppings and sea foam. To the northeast they made out the sloughs where the Napa River spills into San Pablo Bay. Far north, jutting into the sea, they could just see Point Reyes.

Two hundred years and one month after the men of the Portolá expedition became the first Europeans to see San Francisco Bay, a group of Native Americans made up mostly of

California college students led by Richard Oakes, paddled to Alcatraz and began a nineteen-month takeover of the abandoned prison. The occupying group of natives from tribes throughout North America, calling themselves the Indians of All Tribes, offered to purchase Alcatraz from the Federal Government for twenty-four dollars in goods.

In 1989 the San Francisco Giants and the Oakland Athletics met for what would be called the Battle of the Bay World Series. Prior to Game Three, my brother and I sat at home alone, waiting for the game to start. You could hear it coming. In our residential neighborhood semis only rolled the streets when some family moved in or out and the massive moving trucks rumbled. They thudded in your chest, and that was what the earthquake felt like. The shudder grew and kept growing until shelves jackhammered and pictures flew from the walls. My brother cried. I pulled him under our breakfast table and watched our television leap from the entertainment center and dance a jig on the carpet. Then everything went quiet. Not even birds chirped. The heat buckled down as we looked up and down our street: nothing but oak trees and sunlight. Later we would see video footage of Jose Canseco running into home during Tim McCarver and Al Michaels's recap of Game Two till the camera shook into static, and all you could hear was Al Michaels's scream: "I tell you what, we're having an earth—!"

Missions that have been damaged or destroyed by earthquakes:
  San Diego de Alcalá: 1801, damage.
  San Antonio de Padua: 1906, damage.
  San Gabriel Árcángel: 1812, the campanario is destroyed;

1987, damage; 1994, damage.

San Luis Obispo de Tolosa: 1830, damage; 1880s, campanario damaged.

San Juan Capistrano: 1812, the great stone church is completely destroyed and forty neophytes crushed to death.

Santa Clara de Asís: 1818, destroyed.

San Buenaventura: 1812, nearly destroyed by combined quake and tsunami; 1925, damage.

Santa Barbara: 1812, destroyed by quake and tsunami; 1925, damage.

La Purísima de la Concepción: 1812, destroyed. Mission subsequently moved to new location.

Santa Cruz: 1840, damage; 1857, damage; torn down as a result of damage in 1858.

San José: 1868, destroyed.

San Juan Bautista: 1906, damage.

San Miguel Árcangel: 2003, damage.

San Fernando el Rey de España: 1812, damage; 1971, damage; 1994, damage.

Santa Ynez Virgen y Martir: 1812, damage.

The 1812 Wrightwood Quake ruptured the San Andreas Fault in the Mojave Desert and registered an estimated magnitude of 7.5. When the shaking started on that Tuesday, December eighth, neophytes had gathered in the great stone church at Mission San Juan Capistrano for mass, a daily obligation. The church had been quarried from granite, the stones carried over a mile by hand, a train of brown bodies coursing over the coastal trail, massive ants. The vaulted ceiling collapsed, crushing those very bodies that had built it, and forty gave up their souls to God that morning.

Again, on December twenty-first, 1812, the Earth rumbled. At Mission La Purísima de la Concepción de la Santísima Virgen María the *padres* felt the ground shudder and they watched as the campanario swayed then the tiled roof to the church and quadrangle buildings collapsed. The neophytes and priests ran from the buildings in a panic, oaks quaking with the sound of locusts. In Santa Barbara the church walls cracked, nearly coming down. The sea sucked out like a dried pond. Then the water rushed back, a tongue lapping at the shore, and it lapped a mile inland, drowning the mission and destroying what few buildings it found in its path.

The Great Earthquake of 1906 destroyed three-quarters of San Francisco and killed perhaps more than three thousand from the combined quake and subsequent fires. Mission San Francisco de Asís withstood that and the 1989 Loma Prieta Quake.

Mission San Gabriel Arcángel was founded on the banks of what the Spanish named El Rio de Los Temblores, or the River of Earthquakes.

Along with Don Juan Bautista de Anza in his overland expeditions from Sonora to California in 1774 and 1775-76 came Father Pedro Font, a Franciscan, who wrote in his diary of Bautista doling out brandy to his soldiers on Christmas Eve 1775, the darkest evening of the year, a year full of snow. Font complained to Anza that the sin of drunkenness was not a fit way in which to celebrate Jesus' birth. Anza responded that he did not give his men brandy so that they might get drunk, but because the king gave him this brandy to give to his soldiers. Font said, "Drunkenness is a sin, and one who cooperates also sins, and so if you know that a person will get drunk on so much, you should give him less, or none at all." Anza ignored him, and that night Font complained of the men's singing and fireside dancing. Meantime, colonist Gertrudis Rivas gave birth to a healthy baby boy, a boy who would grow up in California, where one day his descendants would live in a region that produces and consumes the most alcohol of any U.S. state.

Christ said, Take this wine and drink, for this is my blood of the new and everlasting covenant, which will be shed for the forgiveness of sins. Do this in memory of me. Yea though, drunkenness is a sin, I assume by its connection to gluttony, as opposed to temperance. Therefore a great sinner am I. By the time of this writing I had to—for financial reasons—cut back on the drinking, but I had already drunk a total of 219 beers, a 750 ml bottle each of vodka, whisky, and tequila, one half bottle of vermouth, nine bottles of wine, mixed red and white. Yesterday, I again jogged six miles, staving off a likely inevitable-at-some-point heart attack.

When Fray Pedro Font and Juan Bautista de Anza reached the end of their long trail, they had come to the peninsula of San Francisco, and Font wrote, "although in my travels I saw very good sights and beautiful country, I saw none which pleased me so much as this. And I think that if it could be well settled like Europe there would not be anything more beautiful in all the world, for it has the best advantage for founding in it a most beautiful city." What would Font say could he drive across the Golden Gate from the Marin Headlands and float out over what

he called *La Boca del Puerto Dulce* on that grand bridge, and
see laid before him the delineated whites of the apartment
and office buildings of San Francisco?

In 1955 Wallace Stevens admitted himself to St. Francis
Hospital in Hartford, Connecticut. There, it's rumored he
converted to Catholicism before dying of stomach cancer,
exclaiming to his priest after the baptism, "Now I am in
the fold."[15] Stevens's late-career poems seem less cynical,

---

15   Maria J. Cirurgião, "Last Farewell and First Fruits: The Story of
a Modern Poet." *Lay Witness* (June 2000).
Peter Brazeau, *Parts of a World: Wallace Stevens Remembered*, New York,
Random House, 1983, p. 295

Archives of the Holy Cross Fathers (Eastern Province) (AHCFE),
North Easton, Massachusetts, 02356. Helen Vendler's letter (dated
8/28/09): "Dear Father Chichetto: I am sorry to have annoyed you
by my putting of quotes around the word 'baptism.' I simply wanted
to indicate by the quotation marks my skepticism about the fact. Of
course, I did find something 'arwy' [sic] in Father Hanley's account, but
I have never accused Father Hanley of prevarication, only of forgetfulness. I believe he believed that things happened as he said, but he
was interviewed twenty years after Stevens' death. Of course I credit
the first part of Father Hanley's story concerning conversations with
Stevens during Stevens' first day in the hospital between 26 April and
11 May. He returned to the hospital with disseminated cancer in July,
and Father Hanley says that the baptism took place 'a few days before his death.' Stevens had not apparently requested baptism in April
during his first stay in the hospital. Of course, I can imagine Stevens
discussing religion with a priest who was attempting to convert him,
but nothing in his poetry or prose suggests any wish to be a member
of any church. It's therefore hard to believe Father Hanley's recollection. And it is harder to believe because there is no written record and
no contemporaneous evidence. I can understand reasons why people
might request that a baptism be kept private. Father Hanley does not
describe any such request by Stevens, so the absence of a written record becomes more inexplicable. Father Hanley, in his long service,
no doubt conseled [sic], consoled, and baptized many dying people.

It seems to me quite possible that he confused Stevens with someone else. Faulty memories are common in all of us, and it does not seem to me at all probable that Stevens would have requested baptism, have requested secrecy, or have responded with the cliché, 'Now I am in the fold.' Such language is inconsistent with Stevens' abhorrence of chiché. I do not impugn Father Hanley's veracity, only his memory. In the absence of any contemporary testimony and any recorded notice, I think that any biographer would agree that an unsupported recollection, voiced twenty years after the fact, cannot be taken as conclusive. There is nothing in Stevens' life and writing that makes a request on his part for baptism plausible or believable. It makes no difference to the writing, of course, which was in any case complete before Stevens' hospitalization. Yours truly, Helen Vendler"

AHCFE, Fr. Chichetto's letter (dated 9/2/09): "Dear Helen Vendler, I didn't expect you to agree with everything I put down in my letter to you. It is disturbing, however, when you ignore the testimony of Dr. Edward Sennett (in charge of the Radiology Dept. at St. Francis Hospital when Stevens was admitted both times) and the Sisters with whom I talked in 1977 (and later) who believed Fr. Hanley's account. They never spoke of any kind of forgetfulness or memory loss on Fr. Hanley's part, whether noble (when one intentionally does not remember injuries, mischief, etc.) or unmeant (when one unintentionally cannot remember things owing to trauma, confusion or some other mental impairment). What provoked me NOT to visit Fr. Hanley in 1977 was their testimony that his account in 1955 was credible and that they believed Stevens was baptized. The Sisters had no reason to doubt Hanley's word, one of whom worked with him and knew him quite well. You seem to want to ignore that. Do you really believe they were ALL taken in by Fr. Hanley's 'forgetfulness,' by his 'mental impairment,' in 1977, when he was alive, retired, and in touch with them? (He lived only a half hour away from them!) Dr. Sennett was too sharp a person and knew the Sisters too well to believe they were being deluded and misled owing to Fr. Hanley's 'memory loss.' Also, in your response, you ignore the fact that a number of priests in the past refrained from recording (in nearby parishes and hospitals) the baptisms of certain dying people. I myself, for example, remember baptizing two people and leaving their baptisms unrecorded on two different more in awe of being and death (read "Metaphor as De-

occasions. That is, I baptized two people (unconditionally and abso-lutely), gave them Communion, and didn't record their baptisms in a nearby parish or at the hospital—for many reasons, not the least being that the dying person wanted no Catholic funeral and preferred that his/her 'reception' remain private (i.e., between himself/herself and God). I mentioned this in my first letter. Such private baptisms did oc-cur in New England and elsewhere! (Today, of course, federal law and new legislation requires that some sort of record of a person's baptism be kept in the hospital as part of the deceased person's medical history. But that was not always the case in the past. And it is anyone's guess as to whether priests abide by those rules today; they pick and chose [sic] so freely.) Finally, to assume that because 'nothing in his poetry or prose suggests any wish to be a member of any church' he therefore could never have requested a private baptism flies in the face of so many 'hour of death' accounts of the dying, many of whose private testimonies, disclosures, groundless terrors contradict the reckonings and calculations erected or founded on their earlier lives (and, in this case, the person's writings). The dying often believe for themselves; not for another person or for the sake of some book they wrote. Any person who has witnessed the dying also knows that they 'say' and dis-close their sentiments (in words and gestures) better than the witnesses or those around them can, foolish clichés and all. In conclusion, I don't think this response to your letter will dissuade you from holding your own belief that Fr. Hanley was forgetful, etc. Indeed, reasoning fur-ther against your opinion in this matter would be like fighting against a shadow—all-consuming, exhausting without affecting the shadow. I also sincerely believe you can't change. As a critic, you have too much invested in your opinion. (One of my colleagues lent me her THE MUSIC OF WHAT HAPPENS to read. In that book you are quite ad-amant about Hanley on page 80.) However, based on Dr. Sennett's and the Sisters' propriety of feeling for Fr. Hanley and their belief that he was telling the truth in 1977 as he was in 1955, I do believe Stevens was baptized privately (though in academic journals his baptism will always be lightly condemned, censured, or laid aside as 'inconsistent' with his writings). I also believe that the baptism should never have been made public. Stevens was a great 'unnamer,' to quote Harold Bloom, and Fr. Hanley should have left his baptism unnamed, as it were, anonymous, like a 'blindness cleaned.' Sincerely, (Fr.) James Chichetto, C.S.C."

generation" from *The Auroras of Autumn*). He could have chosen from at least three secular hospitals in Hartford at the time.

I was reading Stevens's *Collected Poems* when I joined eHarmony and listed that as my "currently reading" book. I fell in love with my wife partly because she knew what it was like to be a literary writer, asking if I was sending my work to literary journals. Prior to this, the first girl I talked to on the phone, when I explained my doctoral exams, said, "So, you're like, reading Stephen King and stuff?" When I said *not exactly* she responded defensively: "He must be doing *something* right, since he makes all that money."

When Juan Bautista de Anza and Fathers Francisco Palou and Pedro Font arrived at the fog-drenched oaks and coyote bush that shrouded the rocky crags at the peninsula's head, the Boca Buena del Puerto roiling below with the incoming tide, Anza dismounted, ordered a cross constructed. He thrust his sword into the damp earth and claimed it for Spain. At that same moment, three thousand miles east, in a collection of thirteen rural colonies, the mostly poor and former British subjects, led by the urbane wealthy, fought their sovereign's troops for independence. A relatively inexperienced general named George Washington wrote to Joseph Reed of Cambridge that the British army had left Nantasket Road and were marching for New York.

Pedro Font mentions all the *yerba buena* ground cover across the San Francisco peninsula south of the rocks of the Golden Gate to the beaches lapped by gentle waves bayside. *Chiropodium douglasii* has been brewed into a tea called *yerba de borracho*—known as a hangover cure.

If you keep drinking you have few hangovers, and no alcohol withdrawal—though this is a rather unhealthy way to live.

Upon reaching Golgotha, the soldiers stripped Jesus of his clothing. According to the primary gospels of Mark and Matthew, someone offered Jesus wine mingled with gall, which he refused. Gall is the digestive bile from an animal. The wine must've tasted awful, so it's no wonder he refused it. Maybe he thought he was being poisoned? Why would someone poison a guy who's going to be crucified in a matter of minutes? Who brought the drink? Maybe one of Jesus' own followers wanted to spare him the pain and humiliation of crucifixion? I'd have drunk that, even if it was the most bitter brew I'd ever tasted. Maybe the alcohol would ease off the pain, even a little. After this tenth Station of the Cross, comes the Crucifixion, during which soldiers gamble for the robe they stripped from the condemned man.

June 27, 1776 Father Francisco Palou, neophytes from Monterey, and two hundred colonists from Mexico, arrived at the shores of La Laguna de Nuestra Señora de Los Dolores. The priest sang High Mass in the fog among the hills just turning early-summer golden. This is the beginning of California's first pueblo, Yerba Buena, which later became the city of San Francisco.

When he learned of the Kingdom of Spain's new ally against the British, Father Serra took up a collection from *soldados de cuera* and neophytes in Carmel and Monterey. He sent the twenty-eight dollars he raised to the fledgling army of former British subjects led by General George Washington.

Junípero Serra opposed the establishment of pueblos in Alta California, for he feared the negative influence of secular life on his neophyte Indians. He wanted to mold Native Californians into his ideal of the Catholic citizen: medieval and monastic, with daily mass attendance and strict liturgical calendar observance.

The Spaniards initially named the Santa Clara Valley San Bernardino—not to be confused with that of southern California. There, Father Francisco Palou's party discovered a large herd of cattle roaming the plain. They wondered where the animals had come from, to whom the herd might belong, and they worried that the animals might stampede, upsetting the colonizing party's own domestic animals. When they drew closer, they saw the herd consisted not of cattle, but of tule elk, *Cervus canadensis nannodes*, elk so large that among those the soldiers shot, they could not heft the carcasses without the aid of their mules. The padre measured the breadth of one animal's antlers at over eleven feet. Shooting elk became rather popular, such that now one would necessarily have to travel far from the Santa Clara Valley, far from the Bay Area, to find a single wild ungulate.

When San Francisco boomed in the Gold Rush, La Laguna de los Dolores was filled. Carriage-loads of beach sand, wood planks from old buildings and sidewalks, rocks and boulders, carted in trains and crushed to level the land where now runs Mission and Valencia Streets crossed by 15th to 19th Streets. 849 Valencia, the offices of *Timothy McSweeney's Quarterly Concern* and *The Believer*, is located where the Ohlone people once filled their baskets with water. At the Phoenix bar I drank beer and my friend went to the bathroom saying,

"I got da poo poo in me, mane." At 740 Valencia is John's Jaguar, a brick garage built at the former location of the Valencia Street Hotel, which sank into the filled land when the ground liquifacted during the 1906 earthquake, and where more than two hundred bodies piled and drowned atop one the other when a water main broke, inundating those who'd been trapped. I doubt that the Phoenix and John's Jaguar are built to earthquake code, but the garage, now more than one hundred years old, is considered a historical landmark.

On June 27, 1776, the same day the colonizing party reached the peninsula and founded Mission San Francisco de Asís, the Presidio of San Francisco, and the pueblo of Yerba Buena, on North America's eastern coast, the Committee of Five—John Adams of Massachusetts, Benjamin Franklin of Pennsylvania, Thomas Jefferson of Virginia, Robert R. Livingston of New York, and Roger Sherman of Connecticut—finished their revisions, and Thomas Jefferson presented a final draft of the United States' formal declaration of independence from the United Kingdom to the Continental Congress. In New York, General George Washington ordered the execution of Thomas Hickey for sedition and mutiny. It's rumored Hickey conspired to assassinate the future first president. Washington also wrote to General Philip John Schuyler, ordering him to put a stop to raising an army of Mohican Indians, because the Congress was unwilling to pay the natives.

Not long after Father Palou settled himself along the shores of Laguna de los Dolores he received as visitors Ohlone Indians, and the padre presented them with beads to show his good will. The native Californians in turn gave to the priest "presents of small value, principally shell-fish and grass seeds." The Franciscan also looked disparagingly at the other native foodstuffs, that he lists exhaustively: their seeds they ground into a flour with which they made a tamal that was evidently very savory, tasting like toasted almond; they ate fish and shellfish from the bay and ocean; they hunted deer, rabbit, geese, ducks, partridge, thrush, quail, beached whale, sea lions, seals and otters; acorns; nuts and blackberries and wild onions. Within a year of its founding, San Francisco's missionaries, soldiers, colonists, and neophytes found themselves in the worst of famines, for the baptized Indians had forgotten how to survive off the land, and San Francisco's notoriously harsh weather prevented substantive agriculture from taking root.

On June 29th, 1776, when General William Howe landed an invasive force of 50,000 troops on Sandy Hook, New Jersey and from there stormed New York City, Mission San Francisco de Asís was officially founded.

General William Howe ordered the execution of American spy Nathan Hale.

In Hal Ashby's 1971 film *Harold and Maude*, titular character Harold, in conversation with his career-military-man-uncle Victor, learns that he could be "working for peace and serving [his] country, just like Nathan Hale." Uncle Victor says that what the country really needs is another Nathan Hale, and that he, Uncle Victor, can see a little Nathan Hale in Harold. Cat Stevens, whose music makes up the soundtrack for *Harold and Maude*, also attended a Catholic high school.

I did not attend a Catholic high school but a public one, because I went to Sacred Heart in the fourth grade and I fucking hated it.

San Francisco de Asís, founder of the Order of Friars Minor and the Order of Poor Ladies, was born Giovanni, named after John the Baptist, but his Francophile-father re-appellated him Francesco. Francesco's mystical vision— à la Blake, that is, Blake's vision à la Francis—of Christ crucified imploring Francis to repair His ruined church, spurred the young man to renovate the church of San Damiano, to the rich kid's father's scorn voiced through beatings. Francesco devoted his life to shoeless poverty, donning robes of coarse cloth. He gathered followers who worked along his side renovating churches. He invented the Nativity display, thereafter to be lit from within, and that now graces lawns across suburbs in America every December. Francis's animals were real. Today they are plastic and hay-proof. Francis reportedly received stigmata after a late-life vision of the Archangel gifted him Christ's wounds. From these wounds, among other ailments, Francesco di Assisi passed out of this life. He is considered the first of Italy's poets.

In 1342 the Order of Friars Minor, who developed the devotion of the Stations of the Cross, took up guardianship of the Via Dolorosa.

Mom walked me, my brother, and sister, through the Stations of the Cross. We did this on Ash Wednesdays, or whenever she thought we needed extra God after church. It might've happened before church, though that's unlikely because we were always late. To walk the actual Stations means one goes to Jerusalem and walks the Via Dolorosa to the Church of the Holy Sepulchre. So the Stations elsewhere—usually paintings, or low-relief sculptures upon church walls—serve as a kind of virtual Dolorosa. Mom held our hands and started from the rear of Our Lady of Refuge: the First Station. Mom said we should say a prayer at each Station and to think of all the pain Jesus went through so that we could go to Heaven. It was hard to keep thinking about that one thing for so long. My mind went to that Saturday's little league game, to the donut and chocolate milk (our after-church reward from Castroville Bakery), and as I grew older I thought about girls. When you're thirteen you can't not think carnally about the girl in the pew in front of yours as she kneels and stands to pray throughout mass, no matter how much God they try to fill you with.

Jesus's real pain, seems to me, would be that—according to the Bible—he never had any girlfriends.

Odysseus had his men strap his body to the mainmast of his ship—crucifixion-like—before passing the island of the Sirens so that he might hear their song and feel the lust but not force his men to run the ship aground.

Crucifixion is an excruciating way to die. Hence excruci-ating: "out of the cross." A man theorized to have been crucified in Jerusalem in the first century—or at least his remains—has a spike driven through his heel bone. Some condemned had a spike extended from the pale upon which they were crucified that sat at the base of the human trunk, forcing itself by gravity into the perineum, anus, or vagina, thus humiliating them while at the same time help-ing to speed their death. The dying shat and pissed them-selves, their waste attracting insects. The eleventh Station of the Cross depicts Jesus clad only in a loincloth. The crucified were always naked. Artists, out of reverence for their Lord, would not undress the man of their veneration. At Our Lady of Refuge, the eleventh Station and the Crucifix above the altar, held a Jesus stabbed and thorn-crowned, blood dripping, and knees scabbed from his three falls.

Despite the primary gospels' (Matthew and Mark) acknowledgment of Jesus' brothers, including the disciple James, the Catholic doctrine of Mary's Immaculate Conception has long forged a view of Jesus' mother's perpetual virginity.

Salvador Dalí returned to Catholicism later in his life and career, after having dabbled in atheism. The paintings from this period—particularly "Christ of St. John of the Cross"—depict the Crucifixion, or crucifixion-like poses.

Victims of crucifixion suffer from exhaustion asphyxia, their hands and arms spread, their chest and lungs flattening so that the condemned must heave their bulk to allow for each inhalation. Then strength fails. Blood loss from prior flagellation with iron barb-tipped scourges and the crucifixion nails, along with dehydration and the ever-present pain contribute to hypovolemic shock. Thus the shortness of breath and exhaustion all reasons for Jesus' last short utterances: *Eli* (or *Eloi*) *Eli lama sabaqtani.* Then death, the day darkening, a raindrop before the storm, the temple curtain torn in twain, the earth rumbling, saints resurrected, eclipse of sun and moon, the heavens bearing Jupiter, Venus, Mars, the Pleiades, Orion. A Roman soldier exclaiming, "Surely this man was innocent."

There's no direct archaeological evidence that Jesus ever existed.[16]

Home, alone, the Playboy Channel shifting into momentary clarity: snatches of breast, glistening pubes, echoes of moans. Afterwards, my stomach sick with the guilt. I couldn't figure out where it came from. Was God telling me that I was a sinner? Was it because I was doing something that I thought was too shameful to let anyone else know that I did it? But I couldn't stop myself. It was irresistible: sex. I didn't care how sick it made me.

Recently, I've learned that the cause of my adolescent guilt and nausea as a result of my masturbation was likely the post-coital refractory period, or Post-coital Tristesse. A condition that affects more men than women, prolactin spikes during sex or masturbation and this causes feelings of fatigue or depression. It's literally "sadness after sex." Thankfully, I don't suffer those feelings anymore, as they likely occurred because my hormones were so whacked during puberty. So it had nothing to do with God or Catholicism, even if that's a better story.

I asked this girl named Buffy to the movies. Mom was late getting us there, just as she was late for church and everything else in her life. Buffy said, "I didn't know we were going to be late." Comments on Mom's temporal inade-

---

16   "There is only an interpreted Jesus, there are many interpreted Jesuses." Meeks. Wayne A. "What Can We Really Know About Jesus? Evaluating the fragmentary evidence." 14 Dec 2011. http://www. pbs.org/wgbh/pages/frontline/shows/religion/jesus/reallyknow. html#ixzz1gWRbXRVl

quacies still rankle her. Mom clicked her tongue, smirked, said, "You could drive yourself—if *you* could drive." Thus began my first date, which I'll have you know went predictably nowhere. Buffy was blond, a year older, a tomboy. She played every sport, and was good at all of them. I never touched her, not to hold hands, not to hug goodbye. We didn't even brush fingers in the popcorn tub. I think what we watched was *The Princess Bride*[17].

While still at Mission San Diego overseeing the rebuilding there, Junípero Serra received a letter from the viceroy praising the founding of the two missions in the port of San Francisco. The *padre presidente* immediately sailed north, for only one of the two missions had been established. Upon reaching Monterey he set out on muleback with Fernando Rivera y Moncada to explore the southern extremes of San Francisco Bay and the plain the Spaniards called San Bernardino.

That plain, now the Santa Clara, or the Silicon Valley, is named on the one hand after the mission, founded under Father Serra's watch by Fathers Tomás Peña and Joseph Murguía on January 6, 1777. On the other hand, the valley is named for the semiconductors created in this same valley, using Si, atomic number 14, atomic weight 28.0855.

What can I say about the Bay? I miss it terribly, while I live here in Georgia. I especially missed it while stuck up there in those humid Georgia mountains. There was no fog, no rolling dry golden hills, studded with live oaks. No

---

17   Coincidentally, Cary Elwes, male lead in *The Princess Bride*, is a Catholic, and has ancestors who worked at the Vatican.

Bay. When I took my wife to San Francisco we drove in over the Golden Gate from Marin. She said, "My God, it's so beautiful!" We'd flown into SF Int'l, but had driven to Monterey, then took 680 to Sacramento, then 80 across the valley to Napa and St. Helena, before finally coming south back to the city via 101. Because of San Bruno Mountain one cannot easily see San Francisco from South San Francisco, where the airport's nestled in a cove that cuts into a peninsula. Likewise, the city only appears when you round a last corner and come onto the bridge heading south: the apartment and office buildings and Victorian homes white and pasteled against dark green lawns, cypress, and pine, the Presidio and cliffs. Coit Tower stands like a fireman's nozzle from atop Telegraph Hill, Sutro Tower towers above the low-hanging fog, enormous rabbit ears. Waves lap the rocks, white with foam. This most beautiful and popular of places to jump to one's death.

Today, Santa Clara and San José could be the same city, as they run one into the other. My aunt and uncle live in San José, in an old adobe where I still often visit them. We sit on the back patio with sunset streaming an ache into our eyes, while tri tip roasts on the grill, to go with the beans and salad. Wine glasses clink. In high school, when I spent a lot of time here, babysitting my cousins, I would jog out to Penitencia Creek Park where children slithered on the lawns like the snakes that still slither in the brome-covered hills.

We skipped down Market to the Embarcadero and watched seagulls land on ships and squabble over old french fries, then we kept on to Broadway and started back up the hill to North Beach. When we got there you said, "My God it's funny all the strip clubs and Italian restaurants," and we turned on Grant after spending hours at City Lights and bought those teas at TuttiMelon and you were overwhelmed because then there we were in Chinatown just like that. At Yee's the chicken was good though it'd gotten cold. We continued our jaunt over Nob Hill and back down to Market and gay men all over asked for AIDS Foundation donations but we hadn't any cash, which was good because it was a scam anyways, we realized, after we saw the same guy hours later in the Tenderloin begging. Maybe not a scam—does it matter?—the guy wanted our money and we hadn't any at all after spending it on books.

My uncle—not the one who is married to my aunt, but her brother—is a gay man who attended a well-known Catholic university, which made my grandparents very proud (the university part). At the time they didn't know their son was gay. That came out later, and Lord only knows what it did to my grandparents' pride.

Among the Ohlone of Santa Clara the padres were astonished to find men who dressed and acted like women. The fathers, investigating, asked other Californians, who assured the Franciscans that indeed some men preferred to be considered as women. Fathers Tomás Peña and Joseph Murguía, along with armed corporals, detained one individual, undressing her to determine her sex and upon discovering her penis forced her at gunpoint to don the clothing of other male Indians, which was nothing at all. They kept the transvestite native at Mission Santa Clara against her will, where as a captive she lived, ashamed of her nakedness. They forced her to perform menial tasks such as sweeping the mission plaza. The depressed native was told that she should not dress as a woman and that she should live among god-fearing men in sin. Then, finally, the priests allowed her to leave. Later reports assured the fathers that her conduct persisted as before. Further investigation turned up *coias*—as the natives called men who dressed as women, and who were the wives of other men—in tribes throughout the region. When the missionary fathers saw two neophyte men—one dressed as a woman—enter a *reduccion* dwelling together, the Spaniards accosted them and found the two engaged in acts that would surely offend a Catholic God. The padres punished the men, though the one protested that the other was his wife, and the Franciscans replied with instructions about the most execrable sin they had been committing. The friars hoped that with the spread of God in the area, such evil and detestable people would be eradicated and in their stead adherents to the fold of the Holy Faith would reign for the greater good of all those native and degraded people.

One of my uncles does not think that my brother and I have actually married, because my sister performed the ceremony for my wife and I, and I performed it for my brother and his wife. Because we were not wed by a Catholic priest, in full mass, we have thus not committed to the Sacrament of Holy Matrimony. This uncle, a staunch and conservative Catholic, is brother to my gay uncle. According to the former, my grandparents dealt with the sexual orientation of the latter, but never accepted it. He told me this at my grandmother's wake. This uncle said: "Granny might have known that Uncle M. was gay, but she never accepted it."

San Francisco has the highest LGBTQ percentage of a city's population in the United States. I was with friends— one of whom had never been to San Francisco, and who wasn't all that open-minded—walking Market Street up from the Financial District. When we got to the Castro, M. whispered, "Just wait until R. sees all the rainbow banners. He's gonna flip." Within two minutes, R. said, "What the fuck is going on around here?" We laughed at his astonishment. R. said, "They have this whole neighborhood?" I said, "It's a *gayborhood*, dude. Big deal." R. shook his head and spat.

My wife and I live in Midtown Atlanta, our city's gayborhood. Atlanta has the nation's third highest LGBTQ percentage for a U.S. city.

I think I was fifteen or sixteen when Mom told me that my uncle was gay, and it felt natural and right, not like some kind of "condition," or illness. My uncle was raised a Catholic, with Granny and Grandpa, and after he told them of his sexuality, it took years for them to adjust to the idea. From the time I'm old enough to remember, my uncle's lover was there for Christmas, the Fourth of July, and other family gatherings. Grandpa laughed at my uncle's lover's jokes, because he's (Uncle R., as I call him, though he insists on being called "Mr. W.") a pretty funny guy. He was simply part of the family. I don't believe my other uncle, my uncle's brother, when he says that Granny didn't accept her son's sexuality. I don't believe that an inability to accept truth was in my Granny's heart. I don't think it was easy for her, but I think she knew that her son was gay and she loved him still. Still, I think she thought that her son's homosexuality was her fault, for unknown reasons. My uncle realized his homosexuality while in high school. He'd been Confirmed. All his life he'd been in church, in Catechism, in a life that told him homosexuality was a sin. He graduated and packed bags for his Catholic education at the prestigious university he would attend. Once out of his parents' house, on his own, he lived his own life. He marched the football field as he played in the marching band.

When I asked my mom about my uncle's coming out, and how everyone reacted to it, she said, "When he told us he was gay, we all said, 'Yeah, we already knew that.'" When she told me and my brother and sister that our uncle was gay, I said, "Well, that makes sense." He'd been living with his "roommate" my entire life. My uncle and his partner (who are now married) have been together for over thirty years.

After the founding of Mission Santa Clara de Asís, near the *coias* the priests so loathed, Blessed Father Fray Junípero Serra, military governor Felipe de Neve, and José Joaquín Moraga recruited colonists from Yerba Buena, and in lands of the Santa Clara Valley opposite the mission, along the banks of the Guadalupe River, they founded El Pueblo de San José del Rio de Guadalupe. Today the City of San José is the Bay Area's largest, and the third largest city in the state of California.

She feared the impending arranged marriage. And what of the wedding night? She was eighteen, unblemished, richly folded in silks. On Palm Sunday the palm in her palm scraped God's spelled name. Clare's father, outraged over her running away, nearly beat her out of the Porciuncula, but Francis himself talked the old man off the poor lady. Saint Clare of Assisi deigned to follow Francis's strict rule: bread, little to no butter, and more work. Her order became the Poor Clares, and her mission, Santa Clara in a valley in California officially named for her, unofficially named for an element—the most common metalloid, silicon—where today God evinces himself in Moore's Law as we inch our way away from humanity.

Now that my brother, sister, and I are adults, my uncle and his husband are openly affectionate with each other, just as any normal, married couple should be. It's never felt awkward at all—at least, not to me. In fact, it would feel awkward if they did not act as lovers in front of us.

I always knew my parents loved each other. Sure, they fought—once Mom hefted O gauge model railroad cars from a display shelf in our living room at my father, a kind of derailment. But what we usually saw, and saw a lot, was Dad sneaking up behind Mom, squeezing her rump, and saying, "Your mother's got a nice butt," while Mom got red in the face and giggled. Okay, maybe that's weird. Maybe for your family that would be weird. Yes, it was *embarrassing*. But it felt okay, like it was supposed to be that way. I did not share the same appreciation for my mother's butt, but it felt right that Dad saw things that way. So it came as little surprise when I was twenty-two and asked Dad to answer me honestly: had he ever cheated on Mom. My dad is good-looking and tall, athletically built, and even now that he's had his stroke he still goes to the gym every day. He worked in Carmel, California, far from Franciscan friars, where beautiful, rich, and abandoned housewives wander the sidewalks filling their shopping bags. Dad probably could've had multiple opportunities. His eyes never wandered. He looked straight at me and said, "No. I love my wife. I love my kids. I'm happy with my life."

I am an insomniac. When twelve and we cross-countried in our Pontiac station wagon towing behind us a used pop-up trailer Dad bought for two hundred bucks from Mr R. in Castroville (Dad still says about it: "a great deal!"), we camped outside Elko, Nevada. Mom and Dad could not have known that I didn't sleep because I never told them; I just waited and waited until the sky grayed with dawn and I could get up, and sometimes I'd finally drift off. Mom and Dad started giggling and rolling in that trailer, shaking the whole thing around like we were in an earthquake. Nausea came up again—not my post-masturbation nausea, but real, actually sick-kinda-sick. I got up to leave. Mom, with her breath heavy, said "Honey, all right?" I lied, said I had to go to the bathroom. And that was where I went for half an hour, in the cold night, and the fresh air calmed my stomach when I sat at our picnic table under the stars and moon over the sagebrush. Summer breezes dry over my pajamas. Now, as an adult, I think of kids with no Dads, parents no longer in love, if they ever were. I'd rather that my dad embarrass me by telling me that my mom has a nice butt.

Before I'd realized what offering Suzanne the empty seat beside me on the bus really meant, I'd offered a movie to her as well. This would be my second date. Seventh grade. Suzanne also went to church at Our Lady of Refuge. Catholic and safe, Mom, of course, approved. Dad said, "She's cute." She wasn't bad looking, even with her glasses and braces, and even if I was more attracted to other girls at school. Still, even if I knew where I stood, it didn't stop me. Despite my chubbiness, I had the guts to ask girls out, and many turned me down. I kept asking because that urge overpowered my sense of shame at unsuccessfully wooing a girl. I cannot remember what movie Suzanne and I saw, but it was likely *Indian Jones and the Last Crusade*, since that was popular at the time, and we could get in to see it since it was rated PG-13, which was exactly how old I was. Mom suggested I walk Suzanne to her front door and there we kissed. Afterwards I wanted to kiss four-eyes brace-mouthed Suzanne again, and I wanted to kiss her all day. So I did, days later, supine on her living room floor, our tongues twisted around together. Her mouth tasted of Doritos. I got an erection, but didn't quite know what else to do, so I kept kissing her.

In *Indiana Jones and the Last Crusade* the hero goes in search of his father who's gone missing and inadvertently stumbles into a search for the Holy Grail, Christ's mythological goblet said to have been used at the Last Supper. Throughout the entire film the Joneses attempt to avoid, but always end up fighting, the Nazis, perhaps second only to Satan himself in degrees of evil.

Prior to Christ's Passion, he celebrates the Last Supper with his disciples, from which the Catholic rite of the Eucharist is derived. Of Christ's Passion, though, the Bible provides no description, as Rachel B. Glaser points out in her story "Iconographic Conventions of Pre- and Early

Renaissance: Italian Representations of the Flagellation of Christ," found in her debut collection *Pee on Water*.

Flannery O'Connor wrote a short story called "Everything that Rises Must Converge," and I first read this story here, in Georgia, where the story's set, and where Flannery O'Connor herself lived and died. But when I read (in the present tense) this story, I think of California, and I think of California.

Geologically, San Francisco and San Pablo Bays are coastal valleys, like the Santa Clara or the Salinas. In the last Ice Age the Sacramento River flowed down from the glaciers that became the Yuba and American Rivers in the Sierra Nevada, through the Central Valley—a vast marshland in spring and summer—and continued into the valley that is now San Pablo Bay. The water found its ocean outlet through a steep and narrow canyon now called the Golden Gate. When the glaciers that covered most of the planet's northern hemi-sphere retreated and ocean levels rose, the valleys became inundated, and eventually they became the great port of the padres' missionary father, Saint Francis.

Among Junípero Serra's and the other missionary fathers' most prized commodities imported from Mexico: chocolate.

Mom would promise that after mass we'd stop at Castro-ville Bakery for a donut and chocolate milk, and that was reward enough for one hour's worth of good behavior.
Waking on Easter morning, just like on Christmas, brought a hunt. On Christmas "Santa" hid several of my gifts in ob-vious and not-so-obvious places, making of the morning a scavenger hunt. Similarly I quested after the Easter basket,

overflowing with fake plastic grass and chocolate eggs and chocolate bunnies, and toys, sometimes plastic airplanes bought by Grandpa, a Pan Am flight engineer. Jelly beans. I was not allowed to eat my candy, though, until after church.

Yet another joke from my uncle via email: An Irishman goes into the confessional box after years of being away from the Church. He is amazed to find a fully equipped bar with Guinness on tap. On the other wall is a dazzling array of the finest cigars and chocolates. Then the priest comes in. Excitedly, the Irishman begins, "Father, forgive me, for it's been a very long time since I've been to confession, but I must first admit that the confessional box is much more inviting than it used to be." The priest replies, "Get out. You're on my side." I have no idea why it's important to this joke that the man is Irish.

In San Francisco de Asís, the natives suffered more than elsewhere from an outbreak of syphilis. Science has theorized that the disease was *re*-introduced to Native Californians, having been originally contracted by European explorers in the post-Columbian era from Caribbean Indians. The disease was then brought to North America's west coast, where the Californians had never encountered it, and thus had no resistance to it.

Treponema pallidum ssp. *pallidum* became venereal in Europe. The bacteria enter a host through an open sore or a mucous membrane and soon produce an often unnoticed non-painful infection site chancre that is highly contagious. Stage II syphilitic infection displays a sore and rashes in the mouth, throat, and genitals. Breaking the skin of said rash area causes spirochetes to escape and re-infect. Along with the rash comes a general ill feeling: head and body aches, nausea. Symptoms can last up to two weeks then disappear. The infected can remain in dormant stage II syphilitic infection for up to two years. Late stage syphilis can lie dormant for up to fifteen years. When onset occurs, the spirochetes violently attack the host's skeletal, nervous, and cardiovascular systems and internal organs. Dry chancres appear on the skin. Eyes ooze a yellow scum and some go blind. The liver shuts down. Then comes insanity as the bacteria attack the brain.

Native Californian women who resisted the approaches of Spaniards were routinely raped.

Native medical practices varied, although many included cutting affected areas to bleed, and illnesses were believed to be eradicated by sucking them out from open wounds, thus ensuring the spread of disease. Indian women served as midwives to both syphilitic fellow Indians, and to the Spanish. Sometimes, while the women giving birth may not have been infected, the midwife was.

The *reducciones* at each mission kept unmarried males and females separated, and closely knit in tight quarters. Leaving the mission was allowed by priest permission only. The women were housed in the mission's *monjerio*[18], which served as a convent to cloister women away from men. In such conditions disease was rampant.

Some California Indians' sexual practices included engaging in sexual activity with multiple partners, thus ensuring the spread of disease.

18   "The *monjério* was an important and necessary institution of the mission system due to the carnal propensities of the Indians."—The Catholic Encyclopedia

The Sacred Congregation for the Doctrine of the Faith stated in a pontifical declaration in 1975, that "the use of the sexual function has its true meaning and moral rectitude only in true marriage."

At least one missionary padre is reported to have entered the *monjerio* nighttimes, ordering the women to sing the *Alabado* while he chose which women to rape. The singing was meant to camouflage the noises of the priest's sins.

Infantile syphilitic contagion was so widespread that three out of every four children born died within two years.

For punishments, neophytes were routinely whipped by priests, opening bloody wounds on their bodies, which helped further the spread of disease.

Congenital syphilis often results in miscarriage or still birth. Padres accused women of purposely aborting their pregnancies. One woman who gave a stillbirth was examined against her will by the missionary father. When she resisted, he had the neophyte lashed, bound, and imprisoned in the *monjerio*. Upon her release the priest had the carpenter fashion from a log a wooden "baby" that the woman was forced to carry at all times, and to treat like a living child—a kind of Pinocchio—as punishment for her "sin." When the woman neglected her "baby" she was whipped.

I didn't think about STDs at all while in high school. I knew about them—it was the 1990s, mid-AIDS crisis—and of course I knew of the chance of an unwanted pregnancy.

But I was more interested in getting laid in the first place than in putting on a condom. Also, I'd only ever seen condoms a few times: used and dried up on the asphalt, packaged and somehow found, only to be opened and blown up like balloons as a joke on Halloween night, along with the eggs and tomatoes that we threw at each other and at cars and houses, and with the Reese's Peanut Butter Cups that I devoured then and still do today.

Date three: I took Amy to the movies. I was not a very creative date-maker. By this time I was a freshman in high school, so still not driving. Amy was in eighth grade, which weirded me out a little, even though she was merely a year behind me; I would never tell my friends about her, but she was more mature than me—sexually, emotionally, and intellectually. She was my sister's friend, which made our families friends, and Amy and I flirted obviously—badly— during get-together dinners and afterwards when just us kids gathered in the bedrooms to watch movies or play games. She always ended up on my lap. Once, while copping a feel, I goosed her and she gave me an encouraging look of surprise that told me those were the first foreign fingers she'd experienced with pleasure. The movie this time I know I cannot remember, because for two hours our fingers crept up thighs and walked inside our shorts' hems. She had me stunned, and worried that others sitting in our row would see us groping each other. But, man, she revved me—*her fingers*. We left that dark theater, cheeks reddened, a little sweaty, her walking behind me because I couldn't hold her hand in that light, and because I didn't know what to do. Brian Beerman, the drunk drug addict who Randy and I had started hanging with (this guy taught us to huff Scotch Guard and to smoke weed, and to chase it all with Southern Comfort, and he was only sixteen years old) worked at that Northridge Mall theater and he laughed when he saw how embarrassed I was with that cute young girl who I think liked me.

Freshman year Randy got into rap and guns. We carried an unloaded .25 caliber semiautomatic to school a couple times. We were that stupid. We exploded terra cotta in the strawberry fields with another gun we'd "borrowed": his neighbor's .32, lifted from the house while Randy was pet sitting. When rap evolved into Randy's love for Nirvana and Pearl Jam, it came with the weed he started smoking. Anyone can see the pattern here. It was still a year or two before Dre's *The Chronic*, and pot wasn't much of a subject for N.W.A. But being stoned fit the Ozzy, Metallica, and Jane's Addiction we rocked. I followed Randy in my own flannel and Baja hoodies. Randy stopped going to his parents' church while we were still in high school, but it wasn't until I left home for college that I stopped going to church regularly, and it wasn't until after my grandmother's death that I stopped going for good.

When the San Francisco Giants won the World Series, defeating the Texas Rangers four games to one, and bringing the Commissioner's Trophy to the City by the Bay for the first time in its 234th year, I went on a good and long run, for the leaves in the mountains on that day were autumn-beautiful and the weather pleasant and warm, with a tinge of cool, and not much humidity.

When Halloween came around while I was sequestered in my cabin, it did so on Sunday, which bothered some of the mountain folk of north Georgia. One woman (a tightly coifed and dyed blonde with round glasses, makeup-less) said, "Halloween should not be on Sunday, because that's the Lord's Day, and the two are really opposites to one another." I did not expect any trick-or-treaters at my mountain retreat, but I did get a bear! A big and beautiful black bear donning a glove with long claws on one paw and a Freddy Krueger mask covering his long snout.

Catholics have traditionally been considered the institutors of All Hallows Day (from Hallow mass) or—in Mexico—*Dia de Los Muertos*, or the day reserved for celebrating our beloved who have passed on to Heaven to be venerated with God. The Church was never a slouch at enticing pagans to convert and so adopted peasant traditions and rituals to bring the heathen into the fold. Some, on the other hand, see Halloween as idolatry, a celebration of Satan and his evil works.

In fact, many do not even realize that Catholics are in fact Christians.

All Saints Day began as a feast for all the martyrs of the Catholic Church, and to act as a kind of make-up day for having missed feast days earlier in the year.

Among films that co-opt Halloween, All Saints Day, Dia de Los Muertos, All Souls Day, etcetera: the *Halloween* franchise, *All Hallows Eve*, *The Boondock Saints II*, *All Saints Day*, *Dia de Los Muertos*, *All Souls Day*, *Day of the Dead*, *Evil Brew: The Legend of Samhain*.

Said movies are products of Hollywood, a neighborhood in Los Angeles, the center of the motion picture industry in the United States. Long before this neighborhood was a neighborhood, it was a town of its own, separated from L.A. by ten miles of citrus groves, and before that it was rolling manzanita-covered hills at the base of the Santa Monica Mountains, and L.A. was not L.A., but was El Pueblo de Nuestra Señora La Reina de Los Angeles del Rio Porciuncula, founded in 1781 by Los Pobladores, settlers from Sonora and Sinaloa, Mexico.

Father Serra first saw the Pueblo of Los Angeles and stayed the night there on March 18, 1782.

"The Dude abides. I don't know 'bout you, but I take comfort in that. It's good knowing he's out there. The Dude. Takin' her easy for all us sinners."

The second motion picture in recorded history was compiled from still shots taken by multiple cameras arranged by Eadweard Muybridge, an Englishman living in San Francisco. The series, titled *Sallie Gardner at a Gallop*, consisted of photos of Leland Stanford's racehorse in motion at Palo Alto, California, site of today's Stanford University. Palo Alto was named such by Franciscan Father Pedro Font in his expedition to San Francisco Bay with Juan Bautista de Anza in 1776. "Palo Alto" refers to a lofty redwood towering from a creek bed, and translates to "tall stick."

The Palo Alto still stands along the banks of the San Franciscquito Creek, down fifty-two feet in height due to soot from coal-burning locomotives rumbling by on the railroad tracks that now demarcate the El Camino Real, and from the lowered water table as a result of the increased population from urbanization. Today it stands 110 feet tall. Who knows what Font might have called the redwoods found north of San Francisco in the Coast Range near the Klammath River, where the trees tower up to 380 feet. One cannot call such a tree a "stick."

El Palo Alto, as the tree's called, is on the city of Palo Alto's seal, and is the unofficial mascot of Stanford University. It is valued at $55,600.00. Meantime, the average home value in Palo Alto, California at the time of this writing hovers around $1.48 million.

The first film shot in Hollywood was produced by pioneer D.W. Griffith in 1910, and called *In Old California*. Griffith also produced the film *Birth of a Nation*, lambasted for its treatment of African Americans, Reconstruction, and the Ku Klux Klan, as well as the film *Intolerance*, which depicted a history of racial and ethnic prejudice.

On October 17th 1874, 115 years before the Loma Prieta Earthquake of 1989, Eadweard Muybridge shot and killed his wife's lover and later was acquitted of murder for committing a "justifiable homicide."

In 1933 the Catholic Legion of Decency was formed to "purify Hollywood cinema." Changed to the National Legion of Decency to reflect its multi-denominational membership, it suffered serious setbacks to censorship after its initial ban in New York on Roberto Rossellini's short film *Il Mirocolo*, which depicts a depraved Saint Joseph who coerces a hallucinating schizophrenic peasant girl into having sex with him. The NLOD's rating system was a precursor to that of the Motion Picture Association of America's.

Saint Joseph—for whom the pueblo of San José was named—was Mary the mother of Jesus' husband and Jesus' acting father. In the Gospels, Joseph is present up until Jesus' twelve-year-old preaching at the temple in Jerusalem. Thereafter he disappears, and is not recorded to be present at the Crucifixion.

The CLOD's successor was the United States Conference of Catholic Bishops Office for Film and Broadcasting, which created its own rating system for films. For example, two movies that received rating A-IV—which are "not morally offensive in themselves, [but] require caution and some analysis and explanation as a protection to the uninformed against wrong interpretations and false connections"—are *The Exorcist* and *Saturday Night Fever*.

My daughter's and my father's birthdays are July first, which is, incidentally, the feast day of Blessed Father Fray Junípero Serra, and—coincidentally—around the same date that the Gospel of Matthew, chapter eight, verses 28-34 are read during mass: Jesus visits the land of the Gadarenes and drives demons who have been possessing two men into a passel of pigs. The passel then runs into the nearby lake where all the pigs drown, prompting the Gadarenes to request that Jesus leave them.

Like Blessed Father Fray Junípero Serra, who forced a confession out of María Pasquala of witchcraft, and collusion with *el Diablo que cargaba el balleton* to kill a man and to attempt to kill Dominga de Jesús, likewise Fathers Damien Karras and Lankester Merrin attempt to command the evil out of the child, Reagan MacNeil, who suffers from demonic possession, evidenced by her spitting, vomiting, fucking herself with a crucifix, talking in a gravelly, evil voice, and cursing. Both priests are killed in the process of the fictional exorcism, which was based on the allegedly real experiences of Robbie Manheim who became possessed in 1949 after playing with a oija board. The power of Christ compelled the demons from Robbie's, Reagan's, and from María Pasquala's bodies, from the native Kumeyaay and Yuma who attacked the servants of God in California, in history, in movies, in Hollywood, through Christ Our Lord, Amen.

The Catholic Encyclopedia states that exorcism has become less frequent due to the practice of infant baptism becomingly increasingly the norm. Thus, "It is only Catholic missionaries laboring in pagan lands, where Christianity is not yet dominant, who are likely to meet with fairly frequent cases of possession."[19]

In *The Amityville Horror*, the Lutz family allegedly asked a priest, a now-deceased Father Ralph J. Pecorara, to bless their new house. It's claimed this priest heard a voice telling him "Get out!" as he walked from room to room sprinkling Holy water and blessing in the name of the Father, Son, and Holy Spirit.

Catholics believe that evil spirits, given power through Original Sin, can imbue ordinary inanimate objects of everyday use. Thus, such objects should be blessed in order to induce in them the desire to serve the good. Such objects are not limited to, but include, "new ships, new railways with trains and carriages, new bridges, fountains, wells, cornmills,

---

19   "Exorcist." The Original Catholic Encyclopedia. 18 Dec 2011. http://www.catholic.com/encyclopedia/Exorcist

limekilns, smelting-furnaces, telegraphs, steam engines, machines for producing electricity."[20]

Jay Anson, author of the book *The Amityville Horror*, once said that his only interest was to write a bestselling book so that he could build a house in Mallorca, and never have to write again. About his belief in the Amityville horror, he said, "I'm a professional writer . . . I don't believe and I don't disbelieve. I leave that to the reader."

The films and books based on *The Exorcist* and *The Amityville Horror* have collectively grossed well over a billion dollars.[21] In *Saturday Night Fever*, diminutive Catholic Italian-American friend to John Travolta, Bobby C, played by Barry Miller (who also plays Raul Garcia in *Fame*), asks Tony's older brother Frank, a recently-gone-lay priest, if Pope Paul VI might grant him and his teen girlfriend dispensation for an abortion.

In *Saturday Night Fever*, Tony's mother always tells him that she wished he was more like his brother, the priest, as she crosses herself. She looks at Tony as a deadbeat and at Frank as a saint. The family's heartbroken over Frank's

20   http://www.freerepublic.com/focus/f-chat/2243090/posts

21   Based solely on Wikipedia's pages and numbers for the following films (as of 2011), *The Exorcist*, *Exorcist II: The Heretic*, *The Exorcist III*, *The Amityville Horror*, *Amityville II: The Possession*, and *Amityville 3-D*, gross sales revenues top $710,059,763. Add to that the direct-to-video releases of 1989's *Amityville 4: The Evil Escapes*, 1990's *The Amityville Curse*, *Amityville 1992: It's About Time*, 1993's *Amityville: A New Generation*, and 1996's *Amityville Dollhouse: Evil Never Dies*, and the books for each franchise, the sales numbers of which can only be estimated after numerous editions, and at least one billion U.S. dollars have been earned by the various entities involved with these two franchises alone.

leaving the priesthood, all except Tony, who sees that his brother is human, too.

To receive an indult of laicization a priest must show that he was psychologically unfit at the time of his ordination. The diocesan bishop then submits the request for indult to Rome where it is evaluated, and if "sufficiently compelling," it goes to the Pope who issues the indult under God's authority.

Many former priests who began the laicization process have already been civilly married for many years, because the Vatican takes too fucking long to do anything.

Frank Jr. tells Bobby C that it's highly unlikely that the Pope would grant him dispensation for his girlfriend's abortion.

Dispensary power lies solely with the Pope, though applications for dispensations and indults are first examined by the Curia. The Pope generally only grants licit dispensations, so Bobby C would've been fucked on that, and it would've taken twenty years to hear back from the Vatican anyway. At the end of the film it's unclear if Bobby C commits suicide or dies as the result of an accident.

In *Saturday Night Fever*, after Bobby C falls from the Verrazano Bridge to his death in the Narrows, a police officer asks Tony if Bobby C committed suicide, to which Tony responds, "There's ways of killing yourself without killing yourself."

Suicide is a mortal sin. To end one's life one must have despair, which is to lose hope, which is to lose faith, thus one will have at that point lost all belief in God.

Sophomore year of high school I started smoking pot and nothing else happened.

I met Sina in art class, junior year. She was an exchange student, Russian, very shy, drew horses. She seemed lonely, so I sat next to her. The color wheel depicts primary, secondary, and tertiary colors and how they relate. Sina and I were blue and another blue. I played football—not very well. I asked her to yet another movie, the old standby that so far had proved nothing. After she'd said yes, but before we actually went out, her host family asked me to scribble down my intentions. I did not write, "I'd like to know what Sina looks like without her clothing on." In the intervening days I'd realized that a movie date might not be as good as a trip to the Carmel Mission. As a Russian, Sina would've never seen it, unlike the girls who'd come screaming into life in Monterey County. So I wrote that I wanted to show Sina a piece of California history, an experience Sina's host family also wanted to own. Neither this family nor I could have seen how magnificently unimpressive our state's 224 years (at the time) of European and American rule were. Sina was from Arkhangelsk, seat of Arkhangelsk Oblast, Russia, a city at least 984 years old, and probably older. I should've taken her into the woods in Arroyo Seco, where I'd once found an Indian metate, and I'd have shown her where the natives congregated and prepared their food and lived and prospered until all these other humans from Europe showed up in California.

The first movie Sina and I did actually see together was *The Nightmare Before Christmas*, a Halloween-crossed-with-Christmas-themed stop-animation film by Tim Burton.

Before that date to the movies, though, at Mission San Carlos I found the bench recessed among the roses and that was where we kissed, her lips balmed, and the balm smelling of cherries. This made her lips oily, a feeling I still don't like. When my wife uses chapstick on her lips and she kisses me, I'm reminded of how I dislike that feeling, but I'm also reminded of Sina, long ago, in the roses.

Sina ended up attending Santa Clara University, a Jesuit College, located on the grounds of lands formerly belonging to Mission Santa Clara de Asís, with the old mission still an on-campus church. After secularization, in 1851, the mission lands were converted to the university.

In *The Nightmare Before Christmas*, protagonist Jack Skellington from Halloween Town accidentally ends up in Christmas Town, where he becomes enthralled by the different environment via his albeit ghastly understanding of secular Christmas traditions.

The first of any real sexual experience came with Sina. We kissed and petted and moved to oral sex. At the time, all that was very exciting, though I cared for Sina in a real way, in that I think I fell in love with her, to the extent a junior in high school can fall in love, when you don't really know what you're doing, except that it feels right and special and real.

I'd split my lip and it got infected, oozing puss and blood. I couldn't smile. I was embarrassed, and couldn't even look at Sina, and certainly would not kiss her. But she wanted to see me, said that she didn't care, that my lip didn't bother her. When I reluctantly picked her up, she said, "It will heal," and she kissed my cheeks and my neck.

Sina and I went to Winter Ball where she wore an almost see-through dress. Before stepping into the Doubletree in Monterey, she scooted across the truck's seat to me, and our mouths met. Her dress slipped from her shoulder, her breast into my hand. Her skin was coffee with too much milk. We made it to the dance eventually, pulling ourselves together, but afterwards we drove out on Del Monte Road, to where it goes straight in an open plain under the stars, where there's nothing but grass and cows and the distant crash of waves.

It grew increasingly juvenile to lie awake at night daring myself to utter a simple sentence. Even if I said I didn't believe in God, wouldn't He know the truth? He was omniscient, right? Even the idea of Him as a him ceased making sense. Not only did this come with a budding realization of my paternalistic culture, but due to the simple question of why? If God was everything, everywhere, all knowing, then why would he be a man? There's that question: If God is a man then God must have a penis, and if so, what for?

Even *Family Guy* depicts God as a graying and bearded old guy with the emotional and intellectual development of a twenty-year-old boy. He's always trying—working pretty hard at it in fact—to get laid.

Confirmation Catechism taught me that upon the Sacrament my bond to the Church would be more perfect. A kind of second baptism, Mom said that it meant I'd be a Catholic for the rest of my life. To have faith meant that I'd committed myself wholly to God, and that faith without work was empty. I still don't know what that last part means, but I have a job. I teach and write, sometimes about God. The Church would likely disagree with what I teach and write, however. I learned that I must have hope. To despair is to lose hope, which is to lose faith. I must have charity, which is to love God and others as I would myself. To show love is to show God—to show faith and bestow hope through charity. Are not these things also work?

The ministers taught my Confirmation class that abortion of any kind was to kill, a mortal sin. Killing otherwise under certain circumstances—such as in self-defense, or for the government, if there's a reasonable chance of success—is not a sin. At sixteen years old—the *age of reason*—the Church ceased to be reasonable. It was not as simple as, *If there's a God, then why is there so much pain and suffering in the world?* The Church teaches that suffering is good, that accepting one's cross in life leads to Heaven. A Church that had "certain exceptions" for inflicting pain and suffering onto others, for example a woman who can not choose what to do with her own body, did not make sense, had no reason.

My sister was pregnant while she stood at the altar during her Confirmation. The Church taught her—as it had taught me—that fornication, the sin of an unmarried woman and unmarried man having sex, was a sin of lust, among the "deadly" ones, an offense against chastity. Through her Catechism and her Confirmation retreat, the ministers warned her against her body's desires, and taught her the murder that they claimed abortion to be. My sister had not told anyone about her body's changes, except her boyfriend.

My sister had already made up her mind: she was sixteen years old, high school unfinished; she was class president, took tours of Washington D.C. as a Young Leader; she had college to look forward to, so that when she was ready to have a child, she'd be able to raise it. Even if she decided to give over her child for adoption, the gestation, birth, and recovery would take her out of school for too long to graduate on time. Never mind the psychological preparation. She knew—absolutely knew—that the only choice for her was abortion.

Roman Catholicism represents the largest religion in all abortion-banning countries: Chile, El Salvador, Malta, and Nicaragua. In Chile the Roman Catholic Church, the largest religion, enjoys privileges from the government, despite the official separation of church and state. In Nicaragua, Catholic bishops often mediate between feuding political entities. Malta constitutionally declares Roman Catholicism as the state religion.

Fetuses are not conscious and cannot feel pain until at least the 24th week of gestation. Over 90% of abortions performed in the United States occur prior to the 20th week of gestation.

On a pro-life website that features "scientific proof" that fetuses feel pain as early as eight weeks, the most recent citation of medical research is over fifteen years old. Meantime, a British medical study shows that fetuses do not feel pain until the 24th week, long into the second trimester, when fewer than 2% of abortions are performed.

According to the Catechism, "Homosexuals do not choose their homosexual condition; for most of them it is a trial."

The desire for sex solely for sex is a sin against chastity. And so: masturbation is a "gravely disordered action."[22]

I can't say exactly how I felt about homosexuality in high school. Other than my uncle, I didn't know any homosexuals—or at least I wasn't aware of any during high school. Some boys were suspected of being gay, which on a rare occasion was whispered about in lunchtime circles. But for the most part if it was present (which I'm sure it was) it was ignored. I never heard anything about any other iteration of sexuality, that is, beyond the hetero kind. Nothing that could ever prove any rumors ever surfaced; I don't think we cared enough to bother caring, to be honet. No one I knew treated anyone suspected of homosexuality with

---

22   From The Catechism of the Catholic Church, Part III, Section 2, Chapter II, Article VI: "2352 By masturbation is to be understood the deliberate stimulation of the genital organs in order to derive sexual pleasure. 'Both the Magisterium of the Church, in the course of a constant tradition, and the moral sense of the faithful have been in no doubt and have firmly maintained that masturbation is an intrinsically and gravely disordered action.' And 'The deliberate use of the sexual faculty, for whatever reason, outside of marriage is essentially contrary to its purpose.' For here sexual pleasure is sought outside of 'the sexual relationship which is demanded by the moral order and in which the total meaning of mutual self-giving and human procreation in the context of true love is achieved.'" Internally quoted passages from Congregation of the Doctrine of the Faith document *Persona Humana* on human sexuality, published 1975.

any cruelty. At least I never knew of any cruelties directed toward them. I suppose we were lucky like that at my high school? But maybe not. Something tells me we'd have been luckier if homosexuality was open and accepted. No one was ever attacked or made fun of. On the other hand, in my memory at least, I don't think that there was an attitude among students that would've been welcoming to a gay girl or boy who wanted to come out, thus no one that I knew of did come out while in high school.

There was one boy who, as a cheerleader, fell subject to suspicion that he was gay. But we were in high school, so of course that's what all the straight boys—especially the boys I played football with, thought of this guy: he had to be gay because he was a cheerleader. But that's it; we just thought it was so. To my knowledge, no one asked him, nor did anyone make fun of him to his face based on this assumption. And he had many friends. He kicked it with all the cheerleaders, so if some guy wanted to date one of those girls (which of course all the straight guys did, because this was like any high school in America), he'd better be nice to her friends. So there was incentive to accept this slender boy with his manicured nails, his effeminate manner-isms, and high-clipped voice, and to treat him with kindness. So perhaps—at least in this particular case—the possibility of an "out" gay boy existed. But, then again, that was because there was something to be had in the deal for the hetero boys.

My sister was driving Granny and Grandpa back from di-alysis and physical therapy when Granny's kidneys began to fail and when Grandpa was suffering from dementia and Parkinson's. Granny had just had some discussion with my uncle and something had annoyed her. Granny said to my sister, "You work hard all your life, you do your best to raise your kids, and one of them turns out queer."

I'm convinced that everyone in my family feels this way: they are sorry for my grandparents for what my uncle inflicted upon them by coming out. I don't think they've ever thought about how hard it might have been for my uncle to deal with his sexuality, his religion, and his family and the inherent conflicts therein.

The Catechism teaches that "every action which, whether in anticipation of the conjugal act, or in its accomplishment, or in the development of its natural consequences, proposes, whether as an end or as a means, to render procreation impossible, leads not only to a positive refusal to be open to life but also to a falsification of the inner truth of conjugal love."

If you have been given the gift of a child from God, giving that child up for adoption is a mortal sin in the Catholic Church. If a married couple is sterile, however, it is moral to adopt "abandoned children." But, the Church—as of the time of this writing—objects to same-sex couples adopting.

In the world's most populous religion there is bound to be varying degrees of adherence to strict Catholic Doctrine. Some interpret the Bible and Church dogma with such strictness that the interpretation supports a patriarchal hegemony. Such Catholics oppose homosexuality and same-sex marriage, do not believe in equal rights for homosexuals or women. Some people bomb abortion clinics. Others oppose the dissemination of birth control and sex education. Some oppose divorce. Then there are Catholics who—while they believe Church doctrine—are unwilling to impose their beliefs on non-Catholics. Then there are Catholics who attend church weekly, go to church on Ash Wednesday and Holy Thursday, and Good Friday, but who disagree with the Church on its stance on homosexuality, abortion, and birth control. Mom is one who believes in a God far more forgiving than the God of Church dogma. These are Catholics who see the truth of the world before them, and some of these never attend mass at all.

On August 3, 1964, Flannery O'Connor, American fiction writer and essayist who penned "Catholic Novelists and Their Readers" and "The Catholic Novelist in the Protestant South," died in Milledgeville, Georgia of complications related to lupus. In her essay, "The Church and the Fiction Writer," she says "If the Catholic writer hopes to reveal mysteries, he will have to do it by describing truthfully what he sees from where he is."

Nearing the end of his life, Junípero Serra had one more mission to found. San Buenaventura had been planned since before the Sacred Expedition, but the intervening years had brought famine, political power play, lack of friars and soldiers, and rebellions against the missions in San Diego and San Luis Obispo. Hobbled from the long-ago mosquito bite, or veinous ulcer, that still plagued his leg, and two years from death, Blessed Father Fray Junípero Serra finally dedicated the last of the nine missions he would found in Alta California.

My parents participated in the Catholic ministry, Marriage Encounter, at Mission San Juan Bautista. They stayed for a weekend, while Granny and Grandpa cared for us. Marriage Encounter's goals are for married couples to learn to grow closer to one another and strengthen their bond. What my parents brought home with them, perhaps more than anything, were t-shirts and coffee mugs, all of them branded with the Marriage Encounter cross, heart, and overlapping rings trademark. But it is true that my parents, for whatever reasons that they chose to participate in Marriage Encounter, lived through and overcame their marriage troubles, and they remain married to this day, a model to me and my wife of lifelong love.

My Confirmation retreat took place in the Gabilan Mountains at a ranch south of Soledad. The hills were scorched summer golden, and a creek ran through banks covered by coast live oaks. Horses canted us up the steep, cow patty-strewn slopes out of which protruded boulders of quartz whiter than white people. We whites ourselves were mixed with our Mexican classmates. My friend Helena's mom was among the Eucharistic ministers volunteering to run the program, herself a white woman who'd married a Mexican. So Helena herself was a microcosm of California. She was big, too, like the state, and full of fury. Sometimes she punched my arm so hard my muscles tightened into knots. We were told that we'd grown closer to God. I remember all this, what I'm telling you, mostly.

French explorer Jean Francois de la Pérouse visited Monterey and Mission San Carlos in 1786 and wrote that the Rumsen and Esselen population at the mission "are in general diminutive and weak, and exhibit none of that love of independence and liberty which characterizes the nations of the north." Pérouse says the Indians are defeatist in their outward appearance, depressed. The native Californians display characteristics common of the despair found among the members of a culture that was dismantled, its practices prohibited. Franciscans shut neophytes away from unbaptized family members. Missionized Indians largely died from disease while the healthy were subjected to forced labor.

Father Palou writes that native uprisings could have been spurred by resentment for the Spaniards' domesticated animals foraging the Indians' cultivated endemic edibles, and at the same time he says that the Californians have no knowledge of agriculture, and that Satan was the agent driving hatred into their hearts.

In 1781, former military Governor Don Fernando Rivera y Moncada, on a missionary and colonizing expedition to the desert of southeastern California, along the Colorado River, encountered Yuma Indians when the natives rebelled against the Spanish incursion, burning Missions San Pedro y San Pablo de Bicuñer and Puerto de Purísima Concepción, missions not founded by Father Serra, but nonetheless administered by Franciscans, and set in place to convert the Yuma Indians, to make them subjects of the Spanish Crown and the Catholic Church. Rivera y Moncada, who had been excommunicated by the priests at San Diego for forcibly taking the leader of the Kumeyaay insurrection of 1775 into custody and out from the Church's protection, was killed.

I chose the University of Nevada in Reno for college. Throughout high school I dreamed of attending the famous

Catholic university where my uncle had gone. Grandpa was always proud that his son went there. Grandpa rooted for the football team, so I did too. My brother and I donned caps, sweaters, and t-shirts, leprechauns' fists frozen mid-air, ready to pugilate. But time with Randy and a pot-filled pipe had taken its small toll. I wasn't that bad a student, graduated with just over a 3.0 GPA, but my SAT scores were dismal. And I was no potential college-level athlete. An acceptance to the aforementioned famous Catholic university wasn't going to happen. But I also thought about snow and looking out from an airplane's window as I soared over the Rockies. I had visited the campus and seen the churches, whiffed the incense. I remembered my stay at Sacred Heart in the fourth grade. In the end I didn't even bother to apply. UNR accepted Californians without test scores if the GPA was over a 3.0. My college would be out-of-state, but a mere four-and-a-half-hour drive from home. Grandpa's cabin nestled in Squaw Valley's pines sat only a half-hour away, near Lake Tahoe where I'd skied and hiked mountains and rafted rivers. Instead of playing sports, I thought I could work in them, and the college had a good pre-med program, and a sports medicine complex. When we visited the campus, Mom saw the Newman Center across the street from what became my freshman dorm. I always told the truth over the phone when she asked if I'd gone to church.

At the end of March, 1782 the foundation cross was raised and Father Junípero Serra sang the first mass not far from the Pacific at Mission San Buenaventura. Father Palou writes that the Chumash Indians in the area were delighted to work at building the first church and the house for the missionary fathers. No mention is made of housing for native converts.

Saint Bonaventure, Seraphic Doctor of the Church, died suddenly under suspicious circumstances after having secured the election in the College of Cardinals of Pope Gregory X. Bonaventure as a philosopher was a Platonist. His writing on epistemology breaks down human existence into three distinct aspects:

Sensory Experience	Reason	Intellect
Under which fall three theologies: Theologia symbolica	Theologia propria	Theologia mystica
Evidenced by these physicalities: Weight, number, measure, memory	Imagination and understanding	Will
Inspiring the following Catholic virtues: Faith	Hope	Charity

Till the end of his life Father Serra would preach, baring his chest to the waist, and battering himself with a heavy stone. He would stab a lighted taper to his skin, spreading the stench of burning human through his church. The drips of gray candlewax blended with the gray of third-degree burns. Meantime the venerable father confessed his sins, telling his neophytes that the path to salvation lay in pain and repentance.

Proposed and ultimately not accepted by the *Diagnostic and Statistical Manual of Mental Disorders*: self-defeating personality disorder (or masochistic personality disorder) is characterized by an individual's desire to avoid pleasurable experiences and willingly enter into experiences that cause pain and suffering, often shunning pride of any kind, and drawing one into self-sacrifice.

It was common for friars to flog, lock in stocks, and switch Indians for "misbehaviors" such as speaking in a native language, being late for or missing the morning recitation of the Doctrina and mass, leaving mission grounds without permission, fornication and/or promiscuity, consorting with women of the *monjerio*, polygamy, homosexuality, transgender tendencies, refusal to labor, and refusal to learn or adopt Spanish customs.

Indians revolted. Father Serra himself wrote, "It will happen that one day, because they are punished or reprimanded, another day, because they fear punishment, yet another day because they have friends over there [where the non-Chrsitianized Indians lived], little by little they will flee there and it will multiply our enemies."

In the midst of rebellion, a young Indian had cloistered himself behind the logs that made up the walls and under the thatched roof of the mission chapel. Seeing the crucifix, he grabbed it and spoke to it using the familiar *tú*, and not the *usted* typically reserved for respect to a personage such as God. Slipping the wooden cross inside his frock he decided that, should he come away from battle unscathed, he would worship Jesus forever. And so: stepping from the barricade of the church, musket balls clamoring and wood splintering around him, he calmly fit, one at a time, his arrows into his bow, took aim, and let them fly. Clouds of dust burst at his feet as the soldiers' aim led astray, and the *soldados de cuera* retreated from this Indian's obsidian tips. He turned back inside the church and fulfilled his promise, serving the missionary fathers for years till he let a final breath sigh from his lips.

One missionary padre fit flecks of iron into the strips of his leather flog so that it would cut flesh. Indians ambushed: one feigning illness to gain access to the priest, the rest crouched in the dark. The reverend Father came on the supposition of performing the last rite, but the natives pounced. The Franciscan pleaded forgiveness, said he would not punish the insurgents. But his assailants ignored him. They first cut away one of his testicles with the rough flaked stone knives of native fashioning, a castration in revenge against the priest for his transgressions. Then they smothered him. They carried his body to his own cell, tucked him into his cot blankets, an attempt to fake a sleep-death. Finally, the men freed the *monjerio*-bound women, and in the orchards the natives danced and had sex until dawn.

Franciscan friars flogged Indians even for searching for food, like Milan, a young man at Mission San Francisco de Asís, who was caught serving his family the clams he'd gathered from the bay's shores.

Archaeology has uncovered graffiti in all of California's missions—Indian pictographs inscribed into the adobe, covered with layers of whitewash. Native deities and depictions of cultural practices show that tribespeople never fully gave up their native traditions even after baptism and coming to the missions.

My freshman year in college I took the required Western Traditions courses. Section I: The Ancient World: where I read the *Epic of Gilgamesh*. My Catholic Catechism could not have told me that the Old Testament story of Noah and the Flood was hardly original, with Utnapishtim predating the Torah by a thousand years. My indoctrination crumbled, a wall that had kept me from the countries of free thought. I hefted my sledgehammer, reared up, and let the blows fly.

The summer my family traveled across country we visited the National Parks: the grizzlies and black bears in Yellowstone and Glacier padded alongside the main roads, past stopped cars, flashers flashing. They loped past our station wagon's windows. Rangers tried to keep the tourists from offering the bears food. Humans are inclined to respond to wildlife in combination, or one, of two ways: feed and/or kill.

As his life came to a close, Father Serra set out to visit all of his missions. In San Francisco, Father Palou was ecstatic to see his old teacher, for the prelate had already written him goodbye, as if they were to never touch one another again. Their joy in each other's company was cut short. In Santa Clara, Father Joseph Murguía fell ill and feared the onset of death, calling Father Palou to his side. Palou writes that since they met in 1750, he and Murguía had had nothing but the tenderest of feelings. Palou hurried south to the mission to see his companion before death overtook him. He must've wept upon entering the religious' cell, seeing the man he cared for drawn thin and shivering on the planks of his cot. And what of Father Serra? Remaining in San Francisco, what could he have thought of this lifelong companion abandoning him for another? All we know is that the Blessed Father busied himself with Confirmations. Blessed Father Fray Junípero Serra confirmed a total of 5,307 to the faith.

The last packet boat full of supplies to arrive in Monterey from Mexico during Father Serra's life brought news that no more supplies or soldiers could be spared for the planned missions of the Santa Barbara Channel, as the *presidente* had so desired. He wrote to the Fathers at missions San Francisco, San Antonio, and San Luis Obispo—those nearest him, both physically and emotionally—requesting they come to Monterey to receive their share of the ship's cargo, and so that their venerable prelate might give his final goodbye.

When Francisco Palou arrived in Monterey, he found his old master indeed weakened. But he was up and singing the Alabanza and the mass, reciting matins, and devoting the Stations of the Cross.

A while back I mentioned a particularly disturbing Cabo San Lucas story, and I promised I would tell what happened. It goes like this: Dad got mad at me because we'd all gotten tipsy on a booze cruise. They have such things in Cabo San Lucas: a boat, free tequila, waves. There were no such things at the tip of Baja California when Don José de Galvez stayed on the beach, preparing the bound ships for the Sacred Expedition. I was drunk and these American college boys said they'd fuck my sister when we walked past them in the street, so I said I'd fuck them up, and Dad yanked me back by my shirt collar to pull me away and prevent a fight from breaking out. He said, "You ass-hole, you want to get arrested in *Mexico?*" Later, calmed, we made dinner plans. Some guys sitting behind us asked what tequila I'd ordered as I sipped it with my lobster ta-cos, and I yelled, "Cazadores!" By now I was very drunk. The restaurant's lights swirled. Dad threw down his napkin and left the table, I assume because he was ashamed at my drunkenness, for my dad's parents struggled with alcohol. And this is what I take away from not only this Cabo story, but from the entire story of this book: I have alcoholism in my family, and here I was in that mountain valley drinking my face off every night.

The opening sequence of the 1955 film *Seven Cities of Gold* tells us that the story is so true to history that the only change the director, writers, and producers effected, was to take the original Spanish and native languages, and translate them into English for the American actors and audience. Based loosely on Isabelle Gibson Ziegler's 1951 novel *The Nine Days of Father Serra*, the adaptation varies widely from a novel that had already taken great liberties with history.

Between the novel and the film, it's hard to know who's tell-ing less of a truth. Ziegler's *The Nine Days of Father Serra* makes no mention of the land expedition's course up from Baja California to the coast at San Diego Bay. Yet Ziegler details the relationship Father Serra somehow develops with a native Kumeyaay boy who speaks remarkably good Spanish, for one exposed to the language for perhaps a year. Meantime, *Seven Cities of Gold* attempts to chronicle some of this journey, with Junípero Serra pacifying a potentially violent band of Indians en-route, utilizing nothing but beads.

Here's what really happened: after Dad left the table in a huff, I was like, *fine, I'm out of here*. And I walked out of that restaurant. At the hotel no one stirred and the darkness closed in from the beach and only the sound of waves skrished the air, and I felt loneliness in me like an empty stomach. I walked the streets and this Mexican from a dusted Toyota said, "Anything you want I got it, amigo." I waved him off. Then something clicked in my chest and my head, something bad, and I turned back, and at the window, I leaned across. I said, "Anything?" I got into this Mexican's car—and became the bear sitting next to him—because I was that kind of big and hairy and dumb when I was twenty-five. He said he had to go to the store. I thought, yes, the convenience store up the street, that's where his homeboy works, and he'll walk in and out and I'm good. But we drove into the dirtied cinderblocked backroads where the people of Cabo San Lucas live—the people tourists spy beachside hawking trinkets for haggled prices. The driver parked, said he'd be back. I said that I wasn't going to sit out there in the dark in that car by myself, and the Mexican guy said, no problem, and he took me with him.

The infidelities to truth in both mediums are multifold. For a post-war novel, *The Nine Days of Father Serra* remains remarkably insensitive to a culturally relativistic point of view.

A contemporary with Salinger's *Catcher in the Rye* and Beckett's *Molloy* and *Malone Dies*, *The Nine Days of Father Serra* is anything but great literature—and was never intended to be. It falls into the action/adventure/exploration genre—practically a cowboy-and-Indian Western. While attempting to maintain characterization, Father Serra predictably despises the thoughts and actions of the lay Spaniards around him and at the same time loves the Indians and reviles their "disgusting puberty rites," and tries to teach them about the "one true God." The natives are always called "savages," and Ziegler writes at one point that "The Indians who lived in the mission lived better than they had in the wilderness."

Father Palou relates a story that occurred not long before Father Serra's death: a band of natives he calls the *zanjones* were reported coming up the Carmel Valley toward the Mission, all of them armed. A detachment of soldiers sent from the Presidio in Monterey came for protection. There were gathered at this time six padres at San Carlos, together there for the eminent founding of Missions San Francisco and Santa Clara. These priests all feared for their lives, but not the Blessed Father Fray Junípero Serra. He kept the other priests up all night with his excitement over what he assumed would soon be his death at the hand of murderous heathen. He told them stories to reassure them, but he talked fervently, expectantly, of his death in the service of his Lord.

How did Joseph of Arimathea and Nicodemus feel while taking Jesus down from the cross? This thirteenth Station—unlucky number for an unlucky man. In Michelangelo's *Florentine Pietà*—said by some to depict a Michelangelo self-portrait in the male figure holding Jesus' body (Joseph or Nicodemus)—Jesus seems to grow out of the marble, rock out of rock. Michelangelo abandoned the project, which was finished by his pupil Tiberio Calcagni, a lesser, and today an unknown, artist. Michelangelo's/Nicodemus's/Joseph's face, though carved of solid marble, looks old and soft as old man's skin, caring for the dead body in his arms.

Wait wait, but I forgot: at the gate stood the first two guards, with submachine guns slung over their shoulders. A third guard in the yard carried a shoulder-holstered nine-millimeter. I knew this was sketchy but I went ahead because I could not walk away at that point. I had to follow through. Inside the cinderblocked cube that was the "store," on the dirt sat the black and white TV going static and then to picture on a Mexican telenovela. This oddly reminded me of the Playboy Channel on my parents' TV all those years ago, though now I would certainly not get turned on, and the cocaine would ensure that. The lone lightbulb swung overhead, no shade. Behind the card table the Man sat, this Tony Montana-ish mountain of cocaine piled. I'm not kidding; there had to have been a half-pound of coke piled on that card table. The Man sweat so bad it pooled under his eyes and his knee bounced constantly. He dipped the corner of a credit card into his mountain about every forty-five seconds and that corner disappeared up one nostril, and the next dip up the other.

Great Christians in Literature: In Robert de Boron's *Joseph d'Arimathie*, Joseph of Arimathea goes to the British Isles and becomes the first Christian Bishop of those lands, founding the mythical monastery at Glastonbury, headquarters of the mission to evangelize the tribes of Britain, and where Joseph of Arimathea kept the Holy Grail that Arthur and his knights quested after in legend.

Father Francisco Palou, Serra's lifelong companion and colleague, stayed at his bedside in the days leading up to his death, hearing the confession of his sins, praying the Holy Viaticum and the Plenary Indulgence of the Order. At one point the Blessed Father said, "I have come under the shadow of a great fear; I am very much afraid." He asked to hear the Recommendation for the Soul. Later that day the *padre presidente* drank some broth, hobbled off to his cell and his bed of boards upon which he lay, his cross in hand, and there Father Palou left him in solitude but for a moment. He returned and found the founder of California dead and staring heavenward.

In the fourteenth Station of the Cross Jesus' body is laid to rest in the tomb and sealed in darkness.

My guy, the guy who drove me to that cinderblock house, I learned called himself "Tony Montana," and I'm also not bullshitting that part. We did the lines I bought and "Tony" asked if I wanted to play pool. It was that or back to the empty hotel room, where my parents and my brother and sister would be, and I was high. So to play pool we went. The rest of that night we returned to "the store" three times, and Tony Montana rumbled me out to a Mexican strip club that was almost as dirty looking as the girls dancing inside.

At some point I realized that I had to get rid of "Tony Montana," and that I had to go back to the hotel, because this guy knew that, as an American, I and my family likely had some money, and something bad could've gone down, because "Tony" did not seem to have any intentions of letting me go. I was able to get rid of him by convincing him that I'd call him exclusively so that he could drive me and my family to the airport. About this I lied. As I have explained: I am a tremendous liar. Our hotel provided free shuttle service, but somehow, as high as I was at the time, I realized that if I promised more Americans to "Tony Montana," and thus more money, he would let me go. And he did.

On a beach near dawn I gifted the rest of my drugs to some high school kids, and I returned to our hotel room and tried to sleep, but instead I watched the sun and tried not to think about how stupid I'd been, how lucky I was to still have my wallet, my head, a relationship with my father to whom I would later say sorry, and he apologized to me too, though he had done little to nothing to harm me and I was only harming myself.

Forever I'll think of that night, and the men with their machine guns, that mountain of cocaine, and I'll still worry my stomach to nausea thinking *What if I'd said the wrong thing? Just one little thing?* And there was the other problem that had to come to an end: that was the last time I bought illegal drugs.

Years later, when the Mexican cartels took control over large portions of Mexico, I was listening to NPR and I heard a story about five beheaded Mexican schoolteachers, only the heads in evidence, their bodies never found. Victims to the cartels who control all that cocaine. I thought about how my stupidity had helped me to grow up, that I had become a cleverer bear. Like most bears, I learn from experience, by failing and falling and picking myself back up. But still, over those years I had contributed to the drug problem that feeds those greedy cartels, and for that I confess my sins.

J. "Grizzly" Adams scoured the Sierra Nevada Mountains, hunting up California Grizzlies for their hides, meat, and tallow. Eventually he captured and tamed them, and in a Barnum-style zoo in early San Francisco, he wrestled bears (his favorite, Ben, named after Benjamin Franklin), and had his head split four times, his brain exposed, and he died of meningitis.

In *Infinite City: A San Francisco Atlas*, Rebecca Solnit writes of the Monterey cypress: "the iconic tree of San Francisco . . . is a majestic form . . . Monterey Cypresses stand for beauty on this atlas's map 'Death and Beauty.'" And yet, the Monterey cypress (*Cupressus macrocarpa*) on the San Francisco peninsula is today a transplanted species. Native to two groves on the Monterey Peninsula, a hundred miles south of San Francisco, the trees have now been planted all over the world. And so it is true that this majestic and beautiful tree is symbolic of San Francisco. But the flora of San Francisco today bears little resemblance to what the Franciscans encountered or what Native Californians lived in over 240 years ago. The San Francisco of Pedro Font and Juan Bautista de Anza teemed with Yerba Buena (*Satureja douglasii*), namesake of the original secular settlement; clumps of prairie June grass (*Koeleria macrantha*) waved in the ocean-blown winds. Along the shores of El Lago de Los Dolores winged water starwort (*Callitriche marginata*) polka dotted the placid water; San Francisco's iconic hills were spotted with coast oaks (*Quercus agrifolia*) and coyote bush (*Baccharis pilularis*); San Bruno Mountain would have towered with redwoods.

The Central Coast of California that I know is today overrun by invasive plant species: English plantains (*Plantago lanceolata*), rabbitsfoot grass (*Polypogon monspeliensis*), common groundsel (*Senecio vulgaris*) more than five different varieties of mustard yellowing up the vineyard rows in spring, and all across northern California's famously golden hills: rescuegrass (*Bromus catharticus*) and ripgut (*Bromus diandrus*); and on the dunes: iceplant (*Carpobrotus edulis*). The plants I'm most familiar with from growing up in California are invasive species.

"Missionization by Spanish Catholics in the eighteenth and nineteenth centuries quickly threatened the languages of Native California, all of which are now either extinct or nearly so."[23]

When we were kids my sister couldn't sleep, not in her own bed anyway. She'd wake at some point after my parents had settled in across the hall and tip her little toes into their bedroom and up into bed with them. My brother and I knew about this not only because we'd seen her through the slit of our bedroom door, but also because Mom and Dad complained about her, said she needed to learn to sleep on her own. And now, a father myself, I can only imagine their frustration, as they'd just reached a point when the semblance of normality began to return to their lives, with all three of their children grown enough to walk, to sleep in their own beds, to know to leave Mom and Dad alone at least for a few hours.

23   See Bucholtz

What they and my brother and I did not know were my sister's nightmares. The two things she most feared: snakes and Jesus. She tells me this today, as an adult, a story of her jog through the vineyards of the Napa Valley and an encounter with a rattlesnake. Likewise, in the Napa Valley, in Granny and Grandpa's house, in the twin bedroom where us kids often slept, atop the antique sewing machine set into the corner, a statuette of a bloodied and thorn-crowned resurrected Jesus. In her dreams, my sister pictured that Son of God standing over her bed. She said, "That dude freaked me out."

Ursus arctoc californicus: California grizzly bear: trapped, poisoned, hunted, forced to fight bulls into extinction. The state animal of California appears on the Bear Flag, large humped muscular shoulders hunching along a grassy knoll. Last known bear alive: gunned down in the San Gabriel Mountains: 1922.

I have never met a descendant of Native Californians. I know not a single individual descended of Spanish heritage from California. Lake Berryessa, near Napa Valley, where my grandparents lived, where my sister lives today, was once a rancho through which flowed Putah Creek. That rancho was once owned by Sexto Berrelleza, a Californio.

Today are restored missions that romanticize a time that lasted maybe ten years from 1815-1825, if at all. Whitewashed adobes, gardens, and fiestas.

In 1846 Sonomans of the Bear Flag Revolt established the Republic of California, which lasted less than a month before the United States took control during the Mexican-American War. American citizens had been trickling in for years, but after 1849 and the discovery of gold at Sutter's Mill, San Francisco went from a village of a thousand to a city of 85,000 people in less than a year. Americans squatted on and stole Californio land, just as the Californios' ancestors themselves had done to the natives who'd inhabited California for tens of thousands of years before them. American lawyers wrested rights away from Californios in the newly-established American courts.

American Indian killers hunted natives. At Clear Lake, California, in one night two hundred Pomo Indians—the lake's native inhabitants—were murdered for "rebelling" against the American settler who had enslaved them to build his ranch homes and to tend to his cattle. The leader of this slaughter, Nathaniel Lyon, is celebrated for being the first Union General killed in the Civil War, the War to End Slavery. Lyon Street in San Francisco is named after him, and he was posthumously thanked by Congress for his "eminent and patriotic services" to his country.

Under Spanish and Mexican rule the native Californian population decreased 51.6%, and while under control of the United States, 83.3%.

The Indians announced Father Serra's death by ringing the Mission bells. The soldiers and sailors garrisoned in Monterey cut away pieces of his habit as keepsakes, for they had seen, according to Father Palou, the Blessed Father's great works. Neophytes, soldiers, sailors, and priests from the nearby missions of San Antonio and Santa Clara and San Francisco came to Mission San Carlos for Junípero Serra's funeral. All told, just fewer than six hundred congregants. From Monterey Bay a packet boat fired its canon every half hour and in response the armed guard at the Presidio fired a volley and in response to that the Mission bells rang out. This carried on for the entire day.

My last mass: my grandmother's funeral. My cousin and I read the intercessions. I screwed up, saying, "Lord hear our prayer," instead of "We pray to the Lord." My uncle's lips turned down, and Father Brenkle looked at me the way a Catholic looks at a pagan.

At Monterey the cattle roamed freely in plains beyond the dunes. The Spaniards slaughtered the beasts in the open air, at shore, where today the Customs House leads tourists out to Fisherman's Wharf. The offal rotted on the rocks and attracted flies and grizzly bears, the bears loping in from the Salinas and Carmel Valleys. They carried off calves when the *soldados de cuera* could not plunk them off with their muskets. Bloody paw prints on the sea sage, and drips into the loamy sand.

Father Serra was a medieval man living in the Age of Enlightenment. During his lifetime, at their best, the mission buildings were constructed of adobe walls and thatched roofs. The large reconstructed whitewashed churches that tourists meander today came about ten years after the *padre presidente*'s death, under Father Fermín Lasuen's watch, Serra's successor. In Serra's time the venerable Franciscan's cell had not even a fireplace. With Carmel's daily fogs blown in from the Pacific less than a quarter mile away, life would have been damp and cold, and one wonders that Blessed Father Fray Junípero Serra did not want it that way. Comfort leads to sloth, among the seven deadly sins. So it is no wonder that in 1786, a mere two years after the prelate's death,

Jean Francoise de la Pérouse, commandeering the French vessels *Astrolabe* and *Boussole*—scientific expeditions, and the first non-Spanish European visitors to the settlements in Alta California—would describe conditions at the mission and presidio as "wretched."

When I came down from those north Georgia mountains I had broken free from the drinking that plagued me. What I have now is guilt. It's a shame I pour upon myself for my poor decisions, for my weakness, and inability to carry myself to health. I think of everything I have, all I stand to lose. I think of my family and all the love surrounding me. In Atlanta, I had my hard drive on my computer replaced. When I typed, I rewrote all of the paragraphs I'd long-handed out in my notebook while in the mountains. And I felt that I'd overcome a mountain, that I'd run up it, and I'd run back down.

Recently I visited home, back to California from Atlanta. The morning when I left I woke up sad because my father had had a stroke. He hadn't *just* had it—it had happened the previous July and it was now September—but that was why I would later fly from Atlanta to San Francisco to chop down three trees and stack the wood: because my father had had a stroke and couldn't work in his yard and I, I decided that I must help my father and honor him, because he's my father and I love him. But compounding this sadness was that I had to leave my wife and two-month-old daughter for two days.

My dad's stroke came while my parents were in town for this child's birth. Dad spent an additional two weeks in the hospital here in Atlanta, not counting the four days we holed up after the baby's emergence from a c-section incision. That brings you up to this day I'm talking about: Thursday, September 22nd, 2011, the day I took a flight to chop down trees.

My morning went about as normal as mornings go around my apartment. I changed diapers and talked to someone who cannot yet talk back. I jogged three-and-a-half miles in Piedmont Park, where work crews hoisted up tents and stages for Music Midtown. The sun beat down but the breeze was fall warm-cool, the way it gets in Atlanta in late September, the best time of the year, when the heat and humidity of summer is dying.

At the airport I kissed my family goodbye and stood in line for security and kept turning, looking back, where my wife held my daughter's hand and waved it for her, so that she could say goodbye and I had the same terrible thoughts I have every time I leave, or my wife gets on a plane on her lonesome: *what if this is the last time I see her*, and since the baby's come, of course now I think, *them*. Movie-like scenarios flashed in my brain: craggy mountains, airplane wreckage, cannibalism.

On the flight, the attendant came over the intercom and announced that they serve beer and wine and cocktails. I thought about the wallet in my pocket, and the Delta Amex card, so easy to use. But when the cart rolled up to my seat and the flight attendant leaned over me, and dropped a napkin on my tray and asked what I'd like to drink, I did not hesitate when I said, "I'll have a Sprite."

When we descended to San Francisco the sun sat in late-afternoon mode, going golden on the Bay Area's golden hills. Despite my sadness about this trip, my sadness about my dad's condition, my unwillingness to leave my new little family, I missed home—California home. After deboarding I stepped curbside and sniffed in the sun: northern California. On the shuttle south, out of the Bay Area, down to the Monterey Bay Area, I passed the billboards and autobody shops of Millbrae, Hayward, Palo Alto, then we came to San Jose and the landscape took on that wider, valley-like feel of the South Bay—what the Franciscans called San Bernardino—and the sun now had almost set. Finally, we rolled over the low hills and canyonlands between San Juan Bautista and Prunedale. And I thought about the Mission there and how long it's been since I've wandered the church grounds or sat on the patio at Jardines over chips with guacamole and I know I won't get a chance to do that on this short trip. I remembered the last time I was at Jardines was that afternoon with Sina, after we'd come down from Fremont Peak, and we stopped at Jardines for dinner. I thought about the photograph, framed and upon a wall in my parents' house, of my dad, me, my brother, and sister, my brother just a baby, and me hanging on to my dad's neck in a kind of play choke-hold, my sister wrapped around Dad's bicep like it's the strongest handhold she'll ever have in her life. I am probably six years old in this photo, yet I remember the day it was taken. It comes to me in flashes: the dark of the carriage barn and stables yawning out of the quad in front of the Mission; the green grass of the quad upon which we all played, tumbling while Dad watched and shoved us around in the playful way that a dad does. I don't remember Mom being there, but she must've taken the photo. But that's the thing about dads: when you're there, there can be almost no one else.

When we reached Prunedale the fog appeared. You wouldn't understand, probably, how someone could miss gloomy, foggy days, but I do. On this fog-swaddled coast, the fog sits—as Steinbeck described it—as a lid on the top of the pot that is the Salinas Valley. And man do I miss this fog. It envelopes the eucalyptus and coast oak and manzanita-blanketed hills.

We exited Highway 101 onto 156 to the Monterey Peninsula, but before we embarked we veered off to the Park and Ride where my mother waited for me. It was going dark; the headlights disappeared in the crowding moisture. We drove to Sea Harvest Restaurant in Moss Landing, a wood shack of a place that juts into the bay at the entrance to Elkhorn Slough and the barking sea lions sounded like they might crawl upon you in the parking lot.

And there, waiting for us inside the restaurant, sat my dad, still suave in his work clothing (for he works selling fine men's clothing) and he had recently returned to work full-time. His dress shirt (a wide striped blue, rust, and orange plaid, woven from Egyptian cotton) tucked into rust slacks, pleated and cuffed and out of style for all but men like my father, a man who makes such slacks look classy. And he was still quiet like he was after the stroke in Atlanta, but he was there. Not much difference, unless you were his son, then you'd see that subtle difference like I did and it would make you sad. And this sadness came because I was watching my father grow old. We didn't know it on that day, but I'm looking back on it now: Dad will drop me off two days later at San Francisco International Airport, and he'll cry, and say, "You're my guy," and he's never done anything like that at all. And I think that he did this because he's suddenly aware of his mortality, and this makes me aware of mine, and of how little time I have to tell everyone that I love them, and to turn everything I've done wrong all the way around.

You could call this a resurrection. I don't think that would be an exaggeration. I cried too, and I missed my California home even more as I returned the 2,500 miles to Atlanta, to my own family, where I found them picking me up after the red-eye, my baby waving hello, just as she'd waved goodbye.

Sources

"ABC 1989 World Series Game 3 Earthquake." 17 April 2012.
    http://www.youtube.com/watch?v=Z8ExMR0c0aM

"Acorns: University of California, Irvine." 21 Feb 2015.
    http://www.google.com/url?sa=t&rct=j&q=&esrc=s&source=web&cd=4&ved=0CDM
    QFjAD&url=http%3A%2F%2Ffaculty.humanities.uci.edu%2F2Ftethorne%2F2Fanthro%2F2Facorn
    s.ppt&ei=9_voVKmNOcqVNoP8gJ.gN&usg=AFQjCNG--s6wVzgYngp1oBfBRUwpnLWe
    NA&sig2=BngdYmTTBv4otwRmQarZAA&bvm=bv.86475890,d.eXY

"Alcatraz Is Not an Island: The Occupation 1969-1971." 13 April 2012.
    http://www.pbs.org/itvs/alcatrazisnotanisland/occupation.html

Amero, Richard. "Christmases in California." *The Journal of San Diego History* 26.4 (Fall 1980). 17
    Dec 2011. http://www.sandiegohistory.org/journal/80fall/christmas.htm.

Bancroft, Hubert Howe. *History of California* Vol. V: 1846-1848. San Francisco: The History
    Company, 1890.

Bardsley, Marilyn. Albert Fish. http://www.trutv.com/library/crime/serial_killers/notorious/fish/
    index.html

Barmann, Jay. "American Indian Occupation Gets Permanent Exhibit At Alcatraz." 21 Nov 2011. 13
    April 2012. http://sfist.com/2011/11/21/american_indian_occupation_gets_per.php

Black, Greg. *Hollywood Censored: Morality Codes, Catholics and Movies*. Cambridge: Cambridge University
    Press: 1994.

Blaver, Angela D. "California Imagery in Context: the Mono Basin Kutzadika's Paiutes." *Indigenous
    Symbols and Practices in the Catholic Church: Visual Culture Missionization and Appropriation.*
    Kathleen J. Martin, ed. Burlington, VT: Ashgate Publishing, 2010.

Bolton, Herbert Eugene, ed. *Spanish exploration in the Southwest*, 1542-1706, Volume 17. New York: C.
    Scribner's Sons, 1916.

Bone, James. "Golden Gate bridge in San Francisco gets safety net to deter suicides." *The Times* 13
    Oct 2008.17 April 2012. http://www.thetimes.co.uk/tto/news/world/americas/article1998161.ece

Breschini, Gary S. "Monterey's First Years: The Royal Presidio of San Carlos de Monterey." Monterey
    County Historical Society. 15 Dec 2011. http://www.mchsmuseum.com/presidio.html

Bucholtz, Mary, et. al. "Hella Nor Cal or Totally So Cal?: The Perceptual Dialectology of California."
    Journal of English Linguistics 35.4 (2007). 325-352. 17 Dec 2011. http://www.linguistics.ucsb.
    edu/faculty/bucholtz/sites/secure.lsit.ucsb.edu.ling.cms_bucholtz/files/docs/publications/
    BucholtzBermudezFunglEdwardsVargas2007-JEL.pdf

Burks, John. "Rock & Roll's Worst Day: The Aftermath of Altamont." *Rolling Stone.* 7 Feb 1970.

Burstein, Patricia and Sue Reilly. "The Amityville Horror Lives On—in a Snarl of Lawsuits and
    Suspicions." *People Magazine* 9.6 (13 February 1978). 18 Dec 2011. http://www.people.com/
    people/archive/article/0,,20070180,00.html

Butler, Alban. *The Lives of the Saints.* Benziger Brothers Edition, 1894. http://www.sacred-texts.
    com/chr/lots/index.htm

Calflora: Information on Wild California Plants for Conservation, Education, and Appreciation. 15
    Dec 2011. http://www.calflora.org/

Calne, Donald B. *Within Reason: Rationality and Human Behavior.* New York: Pantheon, 1999.

Champlin, Joseph M. *The Stations of the Cross With Pope John Paul II.* Liguori MO: Liguori Publications, 1994.

Chapman, Charles E. *A History of California: The Spanish Period.* New York: The MacMillan Company, 1921.

Cook, Sherburne F. "Historical Demography." *California.* Robert F. Heizer, ed. 91–98. Handbook of
    North American Indians. William C. Sturtevant, gen. ed., v 8. Washington, D.C.: Smithsonian
    Institution, 1978.

de Boron, Robert. *Merlin and the Grail: Joseph of Arimathea, Merlin, Perceval: The Trilogy of Arthurian Prose
    Romances attributed to Robert de Boron.* Trans. Nigel Bryant. Woodbridge, Suffolk, UK: D.S. Brewer, 2008.

Deverell, William. *Whitewashed Adobe: The Rise of Los Angeles and the Remaking of Its Mexican Past.*
    Berkeley: University of California Press, 2004.

Diamond, Jared. *Guns, Germs, and Steel.* New York: W.W. Norton, 1997.

Diary of Sebastian Vizcaino, 1602-1603. Vizcaíno, Sebastián. Bolton, Herbert Eugene (editor). *Spanish
    Exploration in the Southwest*, 1542-1706. (New York: Charles Scribner's Sons, 1916). Pages 43-

103. www.americanjourneys.org/aj-002/

Dockter, Dave. *The El Palo Alto Redwood Tree - Arborist Report and Appraisal.* 18 September 1999. 10 April 2012. http://trees.stanford.edu/PDF/elpaloalto.pdf

Drake, Sir Francis. Sir Francis Drake on the California Coast. In, Burrage, Henry S. (editor). *Early English and French Voyages, Chiefly from Hakluyt, 1534-1608.* New York: Charles Scribner's Sons, 1906. Pages 151-173.

Ehrman, Bart D. *Lost Scriptures: Books that Did Not Make It into the New Testament.* New York: Oxford UP, 2005.

Engelhardt, Zephyrin, O.F.M. *San Diego Mission.* San Francisco, California: James H. Barry Company, 1920.

Font, Pedro. *The Anza Expedition of 1775-1776: Diary of Pedro Font.* Frederick John Teggart, trans. Whitefish, Montana: Kessinger Publishing, 2009.

Ferris Bueller's Day Off. Dir. John Hughes. Perf. Matthew Broderick, Alan Ruck, and Mia Sara. Paramount Pictures, 1986.

From Jesus to Christ. Dir. William Cran. Perf. William Cran, Paula Fredriksen, and Holland Lee Hendrix. Frontline: Public Broadcasting Service, 1998.

Gilgamesh. Trans. by N.K. Sandars. Lawall, Sarah and Maynard Mack, eds. The Norton Anthology of World Literature 2nd ed. Volume A. New York: W.W. Norton and Company, 2002.

Glaser, Rachel B. "Iconographic Conventions of Pre- and Early Renaissance: Italian Representations of the Flagellation of Christ." *Pee on Water.* Baltimore, MD: Publishing Genius Press, 2010.

Haake, P. et. al. "Absence of orgasm-induced prolactin secretion in a healthy multi-orgasmic male subject." *International Journal of Impotence Research* 14.2 (April 2002): 133–135.

Haas, Robert Bartlett. *Muybridge: Man in Motion.* Berkley: University of California Press, 1976.

Hackel, Steven W. *Junipero Serra: California's Founding Father.* New York: Hill & Wang, 2013.

Hammond, George P. et. al., eds. *Narratives of the Coronado Expedition, 1540-1542.* University of New Mexico Press: Albuquerque, New Mexico. 1940.

Hansen, Gladys. "Chronology of the Great Earthquake, and the 1906-1907 Graft Investigations" qtd. in *Timeline of the San Francisco Earthquake.* April 18 - 23, 1906. The Virtual Museum of the City of San Francisco. 17 April 2012. http://www.sfmuseum.net/hist10/06timeline.html

Hardwick, Michael R. "Spanish and Mexican California Soldados de Cuera." California State Military Department. The California State Military Museum. 12 April 2012. http://www.militarymuseum.org/soldados.html

Harmer, Alexander. *Don Fernando de Rivera Violates Church Asylum (1776). San Diego Mission.* By Zephyrin Englehardt, O.F.M. San Francisco, California: James H. Barry Company, 1920.

Hoffman, Sarah, Kelly Krug and Vic Tolomeo. California Agricultural Statistics 2009 Crop Year. USDA's National Agricultural Statistics Service, California Field Office. 17 Dec 2011. http://www.nass.usda.gov/Statistics_by_State/California/Publications/California_Ag_Statistics/Reports/2009cas-all.pdf

"Hollywood, California: History and Information." AboutHollywood.com. 17 Dec 2011. http://www.abouthollywood.com/hollywood-neighborhoods/hollywood-california-history-and-information/

Indiana Jones and the Last Crusade. Dir. Stephen Spielberg. Perf. Harrison Ford, Sean Connery, and Allison Doodey. Paramount Pictures, 1989.

Jaws. Dir. Stephen Spielberg. Perf. Roy Scheider, Robert Shaw and Richard Dreyfuss. Universal Pictures, 1975.

Johnson, Paul C., Editor. *The California Missions: A Pictorial History.* Menlo Park, California: Lane Book Company, 1964.

"John Steinbeck - Banquet Speech." Nobelprize.org. 14 Dec 2011 http://www.nobelprize.org/nobel_prizes/literature/laureates/1962/steinbeck-speech.html

Kent, ME. and F. Romanelli. "Reexamining syphilis: an update on epidemiology, clinical manifestations, and management." PubMed.gov: National Center for Biotechnology Information. 22 Jan 2008. 12 April 2012. http://www.ncbi.nlm.nih.gov/pubmed/18212261

Knight, Stephen and Thomas H. Ohlgren. "Robin Hood and the Friar and Robin Hood and the Potter: Introduction." *Robin Hood and Other Outlaw Tales* Kalamazoo, Michigan: Medieval Institute Publications, 1997. http://d.lib.rochester.edu/teams/text/robin-hood-and-the-friar-robin-hood-and-the-potter introduction

Knowles, David. *The Evolution of Medieval Thought.* 2nd ed. United Kingdom: Longman, 1989.

Kroeber, Alfred Louis, José Francisco de Paula Señán, and Vicente Francisco Sarría. *A Mission Record of the California Indians.* Berkeley: University of California P., 1908.

La Pérouse, Jean François. *Life in a California Mission: The Journals of Jean François de La Pérouse.* Berkeley, California: Heyday Books, 1989.

"Legion of Decency." *Time Magazine,* 11 June 1934.

Levy, Richard S. *Antisemitism: A Historical Encyclopedia of Prejudice and Persecution,* Volume 1. Santa Barbara, CA: ABC-CLIO, 2005.

"Manikiki Nation Indian Guides." 17 Dec 2011. http://yindianguides.blogspot.com

Mayle, Peter. *Where Did I Come From? The Facts of Life without Any Nonsense.* Illust. Arthur Robins and Paul Walter. Secaucus, NJ: Carol Publishing Group, 1973.

Meeks. Wayne A. "What Can We Really Know About Jesus? Evaluating the fragmentary evidence." 14 Dec 2011. http://www.pbs.org/wgbh/pages/frontline/shows/religion/jesus/reallyknow.html#ixzz1gWRbXRVl.

Michelson, Emily "Bernardino of Siena Visualizes the Name of God," in: *Speculum Sermonis: Interdisciplinary Reflections on the Medieval Sermon,* ed. Georgiana Donavin, Cary J. Nederman, and Richard Utz (Turnhout: Brepols, 2004), pp. 157-79.

Milliken, Randall. *A Time of Little Choice: The Disintegration of Tribal Culture in the San Francisco Bay Area, 1769-1810.* Banning, CA: Malki-Ballena Press, 1995.

Mitchell, Leslie. "The Man Who Stopped Time: Photographer Eadward Muybridge Stunned the World when He Caught a Horse in the Act of Flying." *Stanford Magazine* (May-June 2001). Dec 18 2011. http://www.stanfordalumni.org/news/magazine/2001/mayjun/features/muybridge.html

Morrisroe, Patrick. "Blessing." *The Catholic Encyclopedia.* Vol. 2. New York: Robert Appleton Company, 1907. 2 Jul. 2013. http://www.newadvent.org/cathen/02599b.htm

Mutual Film Corporation v. Industrial Commission of Ohio. 236 U.S. 230 (1915).

Nabokov, Vladimir. *Lolita.* New York: Alfred A. Knopf, 1955.

"Native American Tribes of California." Native Languages of the Americas website. 17 Dec 2011. http://www.native-languages.org/california.htm

"Native Languages of California: Remission and Revival." [ligvistikwips]: explorations of a developing Linguist. 17 Dec 2011. http://linguistiquips.wordpress.com/2008/05/03/native-languages-of-california-remission-and-revival/

Nunis, Doyce B., Jr. *The Founding Documents of Los Angeles: A Bilingual Edition.* Los Angeles: Historical Society of Southern California and the Zamorano Club of Los Angeles, 2004.

O'Connor. Flannery. *Mystery and Manners: Occasional Prose.* New York: Macmillan, 1967.

Orsi, Jared. *Hazardous Metropolis: Flooding and Urban Ecology in Los Angeles.* Berkeley: University of California Press, 2004.

Orwell, George. *1984.* Signet Classic Edition. New York: The New American Library, 1961.

—"A Hanging." *Shooting an Elephant.* New York: Penguin Books, 2003. 23-29.

—"Over the Rainbow." 18 Dec 2011. http://www.leavingthepriesthood.blogspot.com/

Palou. Francisco. *Historical Account of the Life and Apostolic Labors of the Venerable Father Fr. Junípero Serra and of the Missions which He Founded in Northern California, and the New Establishments of Monterey.* Mexico City: Don Felipe de Zúñiga y Ontiveros, 1787. Translated by C. Scott Williams, with an Introduction and Notes by George Wharton James, copyright 1913, by Edith E. Farnsworth. Reprinted by Applewood Books, Bedford, Massachusetts.

Phillips, Judith. "Alcoholic Beverage Revenue, Tax, and Consumption: A Brief for Decision-makers." April 2008. 28 June 2013. http://www.sig.msstate.edu/modules/cms/images/thumb/258.pdf

Pinsky, Mark I. "Nun's 1960 Recovery May Answer Prayers for Serra's Sainthood." *The Los Angeles Times.* 4 Aug 1987. 15 Dec 2011. http://articles.latimes.com/1987-08-04/news/mn-1302_1_junipero-serra

Pope Silvester II. and the Devil. Chronicon pontificum et imperatorum by Martin of Opava. 1460.

Pourade, Richard F. *The Explorers: 1492-1774.* The History of San Diego Series. San Diego: Union-Tribune Publishing Company, Copley Press, 1960. San Diego History Center. 17 Dec 2011. http://www.sandiegohistory.org/books/pourade/index.htm

Relation of the Voyage of Juan Rodriguez Cabrillo, 1542-1543. In Bolton, Herbert Eugene (editor). *Spanish Exploration in the Southwest, 1542-1706.* (New York: Charles Scribner's Sons, 1916). www.americanjourneys.org/aj-001/

Robertson, Patrick. *Film Facts.* New York: Billboard Books, 2001.

Rodríguez de Montalvo, Garci. *Las Sergas de Esplandian*. Trans. Salvador Bernabéu Albert. Doce Calles, 1998.

Roehner, Bertrand M. "Jesuits and the State: A Comparative Study of their Expulsions (1590–1990)." *Religion* 27.2 (April 1997). 165-181.

Rogers, Nicholas. *Halloween: From Pagan Ritual to Party Night*. Oxford, UK: Oxford University Press, 2002. "Saint Peter the Aleut." 22 Oct 1999. 14 Dec 2011. http://www.umich.edu/~ocf/saint_peter_the_aleut.htm.

Sanders, E. P. *The Historical Figure of Jesus*. New York: Penguin, 1993.

Sandos, James A. *Converting California: Indians and Franciscans in the Missions*. New Haven, Connecticut: Yale UP, 2004.

Sa-onoy, Modesto P., "Parroquia de San Diego." Today Printers and Publishers, Bacolod City, Philippines, 2006.

Saturday Night Fever. Dir. John Badham. Perf. John Travolta, Karen Lynn Gorney and Barry Miller. Paramount Pictures, 1977.

Schechter, Harold. *Deranged: The Shocking True Story of America's Most Fiendish Killer*. New York: Simon and Schuster, 1990.

Schwarz, Hans. *Christology*. Grand Rapids, MI: William B. Eerdmans Publishing Co., 1998.

Seaman, Donald and Colin Wilson. *The Serial Killers: A Study in the Psychology of Violence*. London: Ebury Publishing, 2011.

Seneca, "To Marcia on Consolation." xx. 1-3. *Moral Essays*, V. 2., trans. John W. Basore. The Loeb Classical Library. London: W. Heinemann, 1928-1935.

Seven Cities of Gold. Dir. Robert D. Webb. Perf. Anthony Quinn, Richard Egan and Michael Rennie. Twentieth Century Fox, 1955.

Sloan, Doris. *Geology of the San Francisco Bay Region*, Berkeley, CA: University of California Press, 2006.

Snatch. Dir. Guy Ritchie. Perf. Jason Statham, Brad Pitt and Benicio Del Toro. Columbia Pictures, 2000.

Solnit, Rebecca. *Infinite City: A California Atlas*. Berkeley, California: University of California Press, 2010.

Star Wars. Dir. George Lucas. Perf. Mark Hamill, Harrison Ford, and Carrie Fisher. 20th Century Fox, 1977.

Steinbeck, John. *Tortilla Flat and Of Mice and Men*. New York: Book-of-the-Month-Club, Inc., 1995.

Suaréz, Jorge A. *The Mesoamerican Indian Languages*. Cambridge, UK: Cambridge UP, 1983.

The Amityville Horror. Dir. Stuart Rosenberg. Perf. James Brolin, Margot Kidder and Rod Steiger. American International Pictures, 1979.

The Big Lebowski. Dir. Ethan Coen and Joel Coen. Perf. Jeff Bridges, John Goodman, and Julianne Moore. Polygram Entertainment, 1998.

The Exorcist. Dir. William Friedkin. Perf. Linda Blair, Ellen Burstyn, and Max von Sydow. Warner Bros. Pictures, 1973.

The Godfather. Dir. Francis Ford Coppola. Perf. Al Pacino, Marlon Brando, and Diane Keaton. Paramount Pictures, 1972.

The Godfather: Part Three. Dir. Francis Ford Coppola. Perf. Al Pacino, Diane Keaton, Andy Garcia and Talia Shire. Paramount Pictures, 1990.

The Oxford English Dictionary Online. Oxford UP. 2011.

The Sound of Music. Dir. Robert Wise. Perf. Julie Andrews, Christopher Plummer, and Eleanor Wise. Twentieth Century Fox, 1965.

Tobriner, Stephen "What really happened in San Francisco in the earthquake of 1906." 100th Anniversary earthquake Conference, Commemorating the 1906 San Francisco Earthquake. The Moscone Center, San Francisco. 18 April 2006.

Turner and Hooch. Dir. Roger Spottiswoode. Perf. Tom Hanks, Mare Winningham, and Craig T. Nelson. Touchstone Pictures, 1989.

Ugolino, Brother. *The Little Flowers of Saint Francis of Assisi*. Christian Classics Ethereal Library. http://www.ccel.org/ccel/ugolino/flowers.toc.html

Vatican. The Vatican Declaration on Sexual Ethics. 1976 Jan 22;(4):1-7. PubMed.gov. U.S. National Library of Medicine. 12 April 2012. http://www.ncbi.nlm.nih.gov/pubmed/12266551

Weber, Msgr. Francis J. A Bicentennial Compendium of Maynard J. Geiger's *The Life and Times of Fr. Junipero Serra*. San Luis Obispo, CA: EZ Nature Books, 1988.

—"John Steven McGroarty." *The Journal of San Diego History*. 20.4 (Fall 1974). 16 Dec 2011. http://www.sandiegohistory.org/journal/74fall/mcgroarty.htm

Wharton, Annabel Jane. *Selling Jerusalem: Relics, Replicas, Theme Parks*. Chicago: University of Chicago Press, 2006.

—*The Life and Times of Fray Junípero Serra*. San Luis Obispo, California: EZ Nature Books, 1988.

Ziegler, Isabelle Gibson. *The Nine Days of Father Serra*. New York: Longman's, Green, and Co., 1951.

Zillow Home Value Index. Palo Alto Home Prices and Home Values. 10 April 2010. http://www.zillow.com/local-info/CA-Palo-Alto-home-value/r_26374/

Jamie Iredell lives in Atlanta with his wife and daughters. He teaches creative writing to college students. His own writing appears in many magazines, among them *PANK*, *Gigantic*, and *Copper Nickel*. He was a founding editor of *New South*, and is a former fiction editor of *Atticus Review*. His books are *Prose. Poems. a Novel.*, *The Book of Freaks*, and *I Was a Fat Drunk Catholic School Insomniac*.

OFFICIAL

CCM ◗

GET OUT OF JAIL
∗ VOUCHER ∗

- -

Tear this out.
Skip that social event.
It's okay.
You don't have to go if you don't want to. Pick up
the book you just bought. Open to the first page.
You'll thank us by the third paragraph.

If friends ask why you were a no-show, show them
this voucher.
You'll be fine.

- -

We're coping.

◗

CPSIA information can be obtained at www.ICGtesting.com
Printed in the USA
BVOW02s1732040116

431693BV00003B/30/P